Praise for *Going Horizontal*

"Going well beyond horizontal theory and concepts, this work is social practice in action; a wonderful companion for anyone who senses that reconnecting with our true human nature in our work is the only way forward."
—**Mary O'Keeffe, Director, Loomio (New Zealand)**

"Samantha Slade offers a much-needed alternative to our current systems of organizing. Her book is as refreshing as it is personal and will be indispensable for those looking to bring more humanity into their organizations."
—**Joel Bothello, Assistant Professor, Department of Management, John Molson School of Business, Concordia University (Canada)**

"This book is for anyone who's ever wondered what the future of truly fulfilling work could look like."
—**Melissa Aronczyk, Associate Professor of Journalism and Media Studies, Rutgers University (USA)**

"Samantha Slade—and this book—is what the world of work needs more of. Sparky thinking, applied methodologies, and humanist principles."
—**Perry Timms, *HR* Most Influential Thinker 2017, founder of PTHR, and author of *Transformational HR* (UK)**

"Samantha is on the leading edge of self-management for organizations. She is breaking ground to discover and share the new ways we can work together that we are all starving for."
—**Amanda Hachey, Director, NouLAB (Canada)**

"In the transformation of our society to become more human, Samantha is a reference."
—**Étienne Collignon, President, TeamFactory, and learning systems teacher (France)**

"If there's anyone who knows how to structure workplaces in new, more effective, more energizing ways, it's Samantha Slade. Her book, *Going Horizontal*, is a masterwork in how to turn a sluggish hierarchical organization into one that's egalitarian and alive."
—**Mark Levy, founder of Levy Innovation LLC and author of *Accidental Genius* (USA)**

"Samantha Slade has, with her own life, taken a bold journey into the landscape of how we can evolve our organizations, lead together, and focus on the purposes we choose to serve. I invite you to listen to her, understand her message, be inspired, and enjoy your own practice for a more humane and kinder world."

—Toke Paludan Moeller, sustainable entrepreneurship pioneer, Art of Hosting steward, and cofounder and CEO, Interchange (Denmark)

"Samantha outlines in clear, concrete, and highly accessible language tested practices, ranging from the personal to the systemic, that support participatory ways of working to flatten and democratize organizations. I can easily envision this book quickly becoming a standard reference for those involved in organizational development and change design at every level."

—Rosemary C. Reilly, Graduate Program Director, MA in Human Systems Intervention, and Associate Professor, Concordia University (Canada)

"A brilliant distillation of lived experience, field research, and more academic research—transformed into simple practices to live by. It turns all the philosophical discussions about collaboration and self-organization into incredibly practical and doable practices."

—Caroline Rennie, cofounder of Gen-H (Switzerland)

"This is a brilliant field guide from a practitioner and organization de-signer who has dared to explore, experiment with, and engage with the new ways of working and being. This book must be in the list of essential reading for the #futureofwork."

—Sahana Chattopadhyay, Asia-Pacific thought leader on the future of work and Partner, Enlivening Edge (India)

"*Going Horizontal* is a gift to anyone eager to see beyond the trappings of traditional hierarchy and explore new ways of working and being."

—Brent Lowe, The Scale Coach for Founder CEOs (Canada) and coauthor of *Reinventing Scale-Ups*

"Samantha Slade shares her knowledge and experience with accu-racy, wisdom, and amazing gentleness. This book and the proposed practices are a truly precious help and compass toward more hori-zontality in my organization."

—Damien Versele, CEO, De Sleutel (Belgium)

"Sam Slade's *Going Horizontal* finally brings the notion of cocreation out of the theoretical realm and makes it practical and achievable."
—**Roxane Maranger, Aquatic Ecosystem Ecologist and Professor of Biology, University of Montréal, and President-Elect, Association for the Sciences of Limnology and Oceanography (Canada)**

"*Going Horizontal* is a key piece in the field of organizational consciousness and working transformatively in the 21st century."
—**Melinda Várfi, AoH practitioner and cofounder of Organik (Hungary) and Resonanz (Austria)**

"*Going Horizontal* speaks to the three innate and universal psychological needs for humans to function optimally: self-direction, competence, and relatedness. If you want to increase the probability of having a workplace where fun, purpose, and meaning create a greater good, read this book."
—**Jacques Forest, organizational psychologist; Professor, School of Management, Université du Québec à Montréal; and Chartered Professional in Human Resources (Canada)**

"The time has come for every enterprise to reimagine and redesign how it works, and *Going Horizontal* will be a key resource."
—**MJ Kaplan, Partner, The Ready, and Board Member, Loomio (USA)**

"I especially appreciate the 'how to' approach as this is where you will struggle most when implanting changes that are based on sharing and participation."
—**Bernd Reichert, Executive Director, Executive Agency for Small and Medium-Sized Enterprises (Belgium)**

"Samantha embodies a new way of seeing work and living it, and that is how she has helped transform our organization, step by step."
—**Huguette Robert, Director, and Steeven Pedneault, Social Designer, Présâges (Canada)**

"More than ever, the public sector needs talent like Samantha to learn a basic human skill for our democracy: cooperation for social innovation."
—**Cécile Joly, Project Director, Collaborative Public Innovation and Learning Lab, National Center of Territorial Public Administration (France)**

"Read this book to learn how to see the world in a new perspective and develop a new set of muscles for building the commons!"
—**David Bollier, author of *Think like a Commoner* (USA)**

"Discover how to step into a more mature and responsible management paradigm where human beings can get up to a different level of mastery and purpose alignment. This book has challenged my own beliefs and ideas about my responsibility to be the change."
—**Ana Manzanedo, Governance Connector, Ouishare (Spain)**

"Samantha embodies the principles she upholds: a profound respect of the contribution of each individual and mastery of the science of efficient collaborative processes."
—**Manon Poirier, Executive Director, Quebec Chartered Professionals in Human Resources (Canada)**

"Samantha Slade deeply understands the power and vitality of non-hierarchical cultures. I highly recommend *Going Horizontal* as a tool when developing your horizontal culture."
—**Sarah Houseman, PhD, Governance Researcher, La Trobe University (Australia)**

"With Samantha Slade's book, we now have an insightful resource to help people understand how to operate effectively in this new paradigm. This is the ultimate companion for going horizontal."
—**Edwin Jansen, Head of Marketing, Fitzii (Canada)**

"This book is a must-read, discussing seven domains that are critical in a horizontal context."
—**Ivo Bols, CEO, Irisoft Solutions (Belgium)**

"Samantha's creativity and way of being enliven the collective intelligence methods that she embodies."
—**Denis Cristol, Coach and Director of Training Platforms, National Center of Territorial Public Sector (France)**

"Samantha succeeds in opening up collaboration perspectives that are little known. She reminds us that we are never too small to act."
—**Renée Ouimet, Director, Quebec Mental Health Movement (Canada)**

Samantha Slade

GOING
HORIZONTAL

CREATING A NON-HIERARCHICAL ORGANIZATION, ONE PRACTICE AT A TIME

BK°

Berrett–Koehler Publishers, Inc.
a BK Business book

Berrett-Koehler Publishers, Inc.
1333 Broadway, Suite 1000
Oakland, CA 94612–1921
Tel: (510) 817–2277
Fax: (510) 817–2278
www.bkconnection.com

ORDERING INFORMATION

Quantity sales. Special discounts are available on quantity purchases by corporations, associations, and others. For details, contact the "Special Sales Department" at the Berrett-Koehler address above.

Individual sales. Berrett-Koehler publications are available through most bookstores. They can also be ordered directly from Berrett-Koehler: Tel: (800) 929–2929; Fax: (802) 864–7626; www.bkconnection.com.

Orders for college textbook/course adoption use. Please contact Berrett-Koehler: Tel: (800) 929–2929; Fax: (802) 864–7626.

Distributed to the U.S. trade and internationally by Penguin Random House Publisher Services.

Berrett-Koehler and the BK logo are registered trademarks of Berrett-Koehler Publishers, Inc.

Printed in United States of America

Berrett-Koehler books are printed on long-lasting acid-free paper. When it is available, we choose paper that has been manufactured by environmentally responsible processes. These may include using trees grown in sustainable forests, incorporating recycled paper, minimizing chlorine in bleaching, or recycling the energy produced at the paper mill.

Library of Congress Cataloging-in-Publication Data
Names: Slade, Samantha, author.
Title: Going horizontal : creating non-hierarchical organizations, one practice at a time / Samantha Slade.
Description: First edition. | Oakland, CA : Berrett-Koehler Publishers, Inc., [2018] | Includes bibliographical references.
Identifiers: LCCN 2018024626 | ISBN 9781523095261 (pbk.)
Subjects: LCSH: Management. | Supervision. | Organizational behavior. | Organizational sociology.
Classification: LCC HD31.2.S589 2018 | DDC 658—dc23 LC record available at https://lccn.loc.gov/2018024626

First Edition

25 24 23 22 21 20 19 18 || 10 9 8 7 6 5 4 3 2 1

Book produced by BookMatters, copyedited by Mike Mollett, proofed by Janet Reed Blake, and indexed by Leonard Rosenbaum. Illustrations by Paul Messer. Cover design by Paul Messer/Dan Tesser.

To all the brave souls on your bumpy path
to grow more horizontal ways of working,
in yourselves and around yourselves.
Your personal leadership is building
a better future for us all.

CONTENTS

PREFACE

When I was twenty-one years old, I was studying cultural anthropology at McGill University in Montreal, Canada. In my lectures and textbooks, I was learning about the different ways societies organize themselves and about revolutions. It was the 1980s, and a revolution was going on in Nicaragua.

Nicaragua had received the distinguished UNESCO (United Nations Scientific, Educational, and Cultural Organization) honor for its bold and hugely successful literacy campaign that had increased literacy by almost 40 percent in only five months. The program had become an international inspiration. I was intrigued that this was achieved by educators working with thousands of youth groups. In fact, the country was going through a transformation, and the decentralized approaches to many aspects of the redesign fascinated me.

I became curious to speak directly to people about their experience and understand more. I decided to put my studies on hold for a year, and off I went, on my own, to Nicaragua.

Within minutes of entering the country, I was struck by the mood of the people. The bus was alive with good-natured banter and critique about the new shape the country was taking. There was one other foreigner on my bus from the border, a young man from Finland who was curious about the revolution like I was. People took our hands and, turning over our palms, laughed. If we did not have worker hands, how could we contribute to the revolution? Laughter and loud talk surrounded us. Everyone had an opinion on everything.

At the start of the revolution, it was said that 1 percent of the population owned 47 percent of the land. By way of agrarian reform, idle, underused, or abandoned properties were confiscated. The country debated about how to achieve fairer land ownership. Cooperative farms were growing. Some cooperatives that produced goods and services set up day care centers and social programs for their workers. I volunteered at the day care center and summer school of a cigar-producing cooperative. The impact of the famous Nicaraguan literacy campaign was tangible.[1] The campaign was designed for wider social transformation governed with multiple civil society actors at the national, departmental, and municipal levels. Thousands of secondary and university students and teachers volunteered for five months to teach literacy in rural areas while living and working with peasant families. The program was intentionally bridging socioeconomic divides. A similar initiative was going on in the medical field to bring medicine to rural areas, and a cultural initiative was capturing rural folktales, music, and customs and funneling these stories back into the literacy initiative. The reform was managed in a responsive way rather than being preplanned, making use of a network of 47 shortwave radios.

The new government was accelerating culture with nationwide poetry workshops and culture centers. During this time Nicaragua became the world capital of murals. Artists, both local and international, created outdoor democratic museums. There was a sense of possibility of a different type of country, but there was also a great deal of economic hardship. The economy was out of control, and prices were rising rapidly. The price of a restaurant meal could double by the time you finished eating. War was raging in the jungle. I was trained to protect myself from random armed attacks of the Contras.

Observing these changes in Nicaragua, I gained an awareness that we create the systems we live in, but we can also change them. The organizational and institutional forms we take for granted are but one model, and many more models are possible. I learned the power of decentralized actions and had my first experience of cooperative approaches. The literacy approach and the results it achieved still stand as one of the most astonishing today.

Later, I was drawn to education as a way to improve our society in Canada. I became a teacher, taught teachers, developed curriculum and learning materials, and ended up advising on policy in a Canadian ministry of education. It was a long and rich journey to the discovery that effecting change as a bureaucrat was not a match for me—the ideal place for me to effect change was in fact as an entrepreneur. I wanted to participate in the action.

At the age of 40, I left my government job and co-founded a business, Percolab, that would be a full-on experiment of what a company can be. Percolab is a co-design and co-creation firm that provides support to organizations and ecosystems to step into their futures. It is all about rolling up our sleeves to try out a more participatory and collaborative culture. Each Percolab office is employee managed, and the entire network is self-governed.

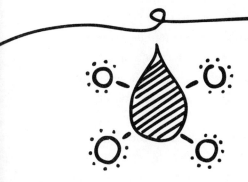

We now have more than 10 years of applied ethnographic observation through the fine-tuning of our experimental operational system and organizational culture and our varied client work in multiple countries. Along with my colleagues and the wider community, I have been making sense of the patterns and the practices that have emerged while living with them and experimenting with them. Beyond the theories and science, I live with and witness the difference that more participatory ways and flatter organizations can make. I have been geeking out, collecting practices and trying them out with teams, clients, and allies for so long that I am full of enthusiasm about all that is possible. Now it is time for me to share. I hear the need and the hunger, for I realize what a unique opportunity it is to have this playing field to try out these practices with others. This book takes all I have learned over the years and passes it back to the field. My background in education and anthropology have been put to more use than I could ever have imagined. Over time I find myself bumping into others, all over the planet, who feel similarly and are stepping away from the traditional ways of doing work and business to create something that makes more sense. People are hungry for resources to help them. It is still a pioneering field that goes by many names. Some call it "participatory leadership" or "collective leadership," others call it "self-managing organizations" or "self-governing organizations," and still others call it "employee-led organizations" or "co-managed organizations." I have chosen to use the terms "horizontal" and "non-hierarchical" for this book. I use them interchangeably. They feel expansive enough to encompass this field. I trust that my experiences, errors, and years of sensemaking can be a constructive source for others.

INTRODUCTION

If you are interested in developing your understanding and capacity in horizontal practices, this book is for you. It doesn't matter if you work within an organization or if you are a member of a group or club or a freelancer or student. No matter what your experience with horizontal organizations, welcome!

This book should help you get further clarity and move forward from wherever you are. The practices in this book can help you step away from fear-based thinking that a plan and control culture strengthens. They help you get back to trusting one another, and they start with you. They help anyone at any level of an organization—from the CEO who wants to take an entire organization horizontal to the entry-level assistant who sees a bright future in this work. Whether you are the CEO or the assistant, you will want to start with your own actions, and only then look outward to the rest of your organization.

It doesn't matter if your organization is well into its non-hierarchical journey, just starting, or even dead set against horizontal ways; this book should be helpful for you because it meets you where you are. The most important requirement is that you are curious and want to learn more. We each arrive to this possibility with different questions. How do you get people to enjoy their work and take initiative? How can the organization be more democratic, participatory, co-creative? How do you keep brilliant team members from leaving? How can your organization embody your values better? At one point the questions become more personal. What do I want it to be in this team, this organization, this community? How am I moving this forward? This book is not about examining what is wrong with your organization or your colleagues; instead, it is about your own non-hierarchical mind-set and ways. How are *you* embodying non-hierarchical practices, and where can they deepen and expand?

Everywhere I go, when I talk about how we have cornered ourselves into habits and ways of working, ways that don't make sense, people nod in agreement. Rarely does that statement get challenged. When I add, "and we are not quite sure how to move things along," the nod is even more emphatic. It's an acknowledgment that something is amiss in our organizations and that we are confused about finding a path forward. This book offers supportive frameworks to help you get beyond the current hierarchical culture we have become accustomed to. The practices and structures in this book will help you cultivate and grow non-hierarchical culture in your organization. By starting with yourself, you can give space and opportunity to grow the non-hierarchical ways in others around you.

The book is organized into chapters on the seven domains of practice that are common to most all organizations: autonomy, purpose, meetings, transparency, decision making, learning and development, and relationships and conflict. In each of these chapters, I explain why the domain of practice is critical to horizontal organizations and mind-set, I offer ways to recognize how similar horizontal practices might be

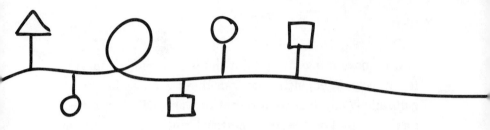

showing up in your life outside of work, and I lay out some foundational practices of each domain that you can start using in your organization right away. Throughout the book you are invited to do regular exercises that will help you take the practices into your organizational context—mapping your organizational culture, reflecting on how you would want to be functioning, and exploring possibilities around you.

The book includes a sprinkling of models and theory to ground the work. The final chapter serves to guide you into strategic actions for your specific organizational context and requires that you have read all the preceding chapters. There is an order to the practice domains that are presented in the book, as together they constitute a comprehensive path into horizontal habits. At the same time, if a particular domain is pulling you in, know that each chapter stands on its own and you can jump back and forth. This book helps you develop new ways of seeing the daily details of your organization and how you do things, understand the differences between behaviors that support a hierarchical or non-hierarchical mindset, and look at the complexity those behaviors interconnect with.

You will find ways to try out new behaviors for yourself and with others. Maybe you will start outside of work or in informal groups before you bring them into work. Maybe you have perfect opportunities right in front of you that this book will help you see. The idea is to start small with consciousness and then to grow and widen, always keeping the focus on lived experience. One thing that you will need to be uncompromising about is the following: *you* are the prototype space. Stop proposing for others and start with yourself.

Chances are, you will be both validated and challenged in things that you are doing. We do not need to wait for some higher authority to give us permission to embark on a non-hierarchical journey. The journey starts with each of us. This is everyone's work. Many books target leaders, and that is important because leaders have the power to change the organizational structure. However, because a horizontal culture includes everyone, this book speaks to everyone in the organization.

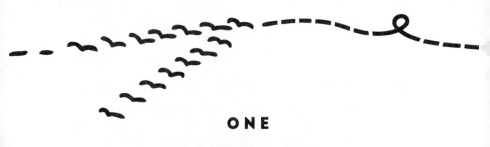

ONE

WHY GO HORIZONTAL?

*There is no need to wait for permission from hierarchy
to begin practicing non-hierarchical ways.*

Human Nature Is Non-hierarchical

Non-hierarchical ways are the modus operandi of human beings. They are part of our DNA. Like geese flying south and bears hibernating, we are a self-organizing species.

We function every day without a boss. We feed ourselves, keep up our homes, care for each other, plan big projects, celebrate victories, and mourn losses. Every day, we organize ourselves with those around us, adult to adult. We figure things out together. Most of the time, we appreciate the input and support others offer. When that support tips into telling us what to do, we get wary. We are properly allergic to the notion that someone could have the power over us to make us do something we don't want to do. For the most part, we figure out how to work with different opinions, preferences, and perspectives. We manage to accomplish things together, whether it is building a snowman or organizing a birthday party. If a friend or partner tries to "manage" what we do, decide, or think, that can compromise the relationship. We tend to stay in our various communities as long as they are non-hierarchical. Simply put, we need horizontal workplaces because we are naturally a horizontal species. Working against this instinct is what has lead us to a world where 85 percent of people are disengaged from their work, *work* itself is a negative word, and movies like *Office Space* become cult classics of catharsis. We can do better!

In my workshops I ask participants to identify examples from their personal lives where they figure things out with others, without anyone having authority over another. We don't tend to think about our world in this way. People really struggle to find examples, though in reality they abound: we decide what music is played in the house, we get groceries for the house, we get married to whom we want. We cross paths with people we know and don't know at the grocery store, the swimming pool, the park, without anyone telling us what to do. There is no chain of command in daily life. This is not to say that it is easy, but I think it is fair to say we wouldn't want it any other way. The other way is the making of science fiction scenarios.

Non-hierarchical Ways Are Possible and Present in the Workplace

Despite human nature being horizontal, the organizational model and culture we have given ourselves for work is vertical. Of course, you can't just take non-hierarchical ways from the personal realm into the work realm. There are some fundamental differences that need to be taken into account. At work we are contractually tied to our organizations through formal agreements that we are bound to. We receive regular paychecks that we rely upon. We are accountable to the organization and its purpose. We are under pressure to perform and ensure financial viability. We must adhere to a whole body of legal requirements.

While our organizations could have developed in non-hierarchical ways, and there are many examples of non-hierarchical societies throughout history and across cultures, the model that prevailed was a vertical one. Some might say it was for the sake of efficiency and scale, though there are examples of efficient large-scale non-hierarchical organizations. Others might point out that it was a model that supported the extractive and colonialist values of earlier times. Certainly, human well-being was not the focus at the origins of the hierarchical organizational model. The result today is such that the current dominant organizational culture and structure is not aligned to human nature.

When I am brought into an organization to help them with this transition, I often hear things like "This organizational chart might look vertical, but really we invite you to talk to people in the company as if it were horizontal." Or, from someone in upper management, "I'm not really the boss; people don't even use that term with me." This is not going horizontal; it is hierarchy that likes to pretend that it is not, that pays lip service to the concept without doing the real shift.

When I speak to people who truly love their work, they say things like "My boss trusts me" or "I have freedom to do what I want" or "I'm encouraged to try things out." All these statements are elements of more human, natural ways of functioning whereby people feel like they are being treated with mutual trust and care, as adults. In many places human beings are being treated fairly as equals despite the vertical culture. In many other places, just the opposite is true. You know where you stand with your own stories and experiences.

Hierarchy Won't Take Us into Our Future

The 9 to 5 office with the hierarchical organizational chart is showing serious signs of fraying. The dominant management model is expensive. Management experts Gary Hamel and Michele Zanini estimate that the cost of micromanagement is $3 trillion annually in the United States alone.[2] The human cost is also alarming. Worker engagement is not getting better despite the billion-dollar industry making efforts to effect improvement. Only 15 percent of the world's workforce are actively engaged in their jobs.[3]

The major sources of psychological distress in the workplace are connected to hierarchical culture: poor relationship with one's superior, lack of recognition, and low participation in decision making and governance.[4] Furthermore, organizations are struggling to attract and keep employees. High-talent individuals are leaving the workplace to seek out greater learning and development.[5] Organizations face workforce challenges that are a serious issue and a growing trend. This trend touches me deeply. Human suffering increases with our current model.

In the meantime we are entering a new era. We are finding a general nonacceptance of many organizational practices that used to be tolerated: from inequity in pay to rigid rules. Professionals are honing their personal brands and positioning themselves for a market in which employers are competing among themselves to hire them. The freelance market continues to grow and organize into collectives to provide shared services and social safety nets usually offered by employers.[6] Networked organizations are growing. A parallel infrastructure of co-working networks and wholly decentralized companies is growing for digital nomads and location-independent workers who care about freedom and beauty in their workspace. The upcoming workforce is connected to so much information, possibility, and creativity that the traditional vertical organizational system seems under-equipped to tap into its full potential.[7] The internet mind-set is not a hierarchical mind-set. Millennials do not understand why information and authority cannot be dynamic and flow-ing. When an organization shifts to a transparent culture of shared power and mutual responsibility and care, then it can truly begin to respond to the challenges modern organiza-tions are facing. A recent report on the future of organiza-tions concludes that the ability to "scale trust" is key for the organization of the future to offer space for the new worker.[8]

Artificial intelligence is poised to shake our work world. Some say 40 percent of today's jobs will disappear.[9] We know that the obedience and compliance mind-set that standard-ization bred will need to give way to empathy, creativity, and real-time decision making, for example. These capacities are valued and thrive in horizontal cultures.

Depending on your perspective, all this can be an invi-tation, an opportunity, or a wake-up call to revisit what we have been taking for granted in the way our organizations function. The work is deeper than we might have envisioned; it requires new mind-sets, new personal and collective prac-tices, and new organizational models. There are no recipes for the depth of what it involves. It is beyond an issue of pro-ductivity; it speaks to the question of how we want to be together as human beings.

Non-hierarchical ways are needed for a future functioning organizational culture, and they are well positioned for the expectations and culture of the upcoming generation.

What Does a Successful Horizontal Organizational Mind-Set Look Like?

Horizontal ways deal with the pervasive and detrimental issue of organizational disengagement and positively contribute to the mental well-being of humans. When humans are taken care of, they get things done, and that is what organizations need: to stay in movement, to stay ahead, to stay relevant. Let's look at some specifics: when we say employees are more engaged, what does that mean? Here are some traits that show the difference:

Disengaged worker	Engaged worker
Executes tasks, avoids work	Shows up and works with spirit and care
Has little desire to learn new things	Is curious and proactive to grow and develop
Complains, blames, victimizes	Contributes ideas, offers support for others
Shows indifference toward colleagues	Invests in colleagues and relationships
Shows indifference toward the organization's success	Imagines possibilities, co-creates, proposes

Buurtzorg is a home-care company in the Netherlands that was created in 2007 with a horizontal structure. The organization is based on trust and works with small teams of 10 to 12 nurses who have the authority to do what would usually be done at the management level—human resources functions, budgeting, scheduling, and performance reviews. A central office of 50 people supports (not manages) the 14,000 nurses. After seven years of existence, Buurtzorg had taken two-thirds of the market in the Netherlands. Today, Buurtzorg is expanding around the world to countries such as the United Kingdom, the United States, Japan, and China. The organization has been the subject of studies that demonstrate how it is a success in achieving high levels of client satisfaction, employee well-being, and profitability.[10]

Here are five indicators of a successful non-hierarchical organization. Keep in mind that this is the gold standard; these metrics can take years of small iterative changes to achieve.

1. Colleagues Hold Each Other Accountable, and Responsibility Is Shared.

Some people think a that non-hierarchical mind-set means no management at all. The reality is quite the opposite: a non-hierarchical mind-set holds everyone to a higher standard.

Many activities that managers once were responsible for are distributed, and thus the responsibility becomes shared. A whole team participates in the activities that a single manager would usually hold: setting objectives, organizing work to be done, setting pay, supporting and motivating one another, holding one another accountable to performance, and supporting one another's development.

2. People Own Their Personal Leadership.

The premise of a horizontal mind-set is that people can figure things out for themselves, among themselves. There is no need to have someone with authority give permission or approval or do things on behalf of others. We have come to think of leaders as those persons at the top of the organization. This association is false. A non-hierarchical mind-set is about owning our personal leadership no matter where we might be positioned in an organization, no matter the nature of our work. If we see something not working, we act on it. We take care of things, and we make proposals.

3. People Do Not Feel Imposed Upon, and Yet They Honor Their Commitments.

People do not feel imposed upon by one another in a horizontal organization. This does *not* mean people do whatever they want. Understanding this requires nuance. In some cases authority should be distributed and a group will decide things together, and in other cases the group's interest is best served when someone decides for the group (like when a seaplane pilot tells passengers the safe spots to sit in a plane). For a horizontal mind-set to work, people must honor their commitments, or else they will be im-

posing on their peers. It is the very empowerment of feeling ownership of the process that inspires people to honor those commitments.

4. Actions Are Both Participatory and Responsive.

Horizontal does not mean chaos! Successful non-hierarchical culture is both participatory and responsive. Things get done. We are hardwired to think that opening up processes to a wider group adds time and pain. Of course, if you open up the responsibilities without thoughtful process, things will not get done. Many of us have experienced that. Non-hierarchical  ways replace this free-for-all with structures that are proven to manage participatory culture smoothly. As the chain of command is lifted, the hierarchical structures are replaced by lighter, less hierarchical structures: roles with purpose, accountabilities, and metrics that matter; decision-making methods and spaces that are explicit; meetings that are well documented; people who are aware of what everyone else is doing; mechanisms that strengthen relationships, and work through conflicts. With successful self-organization, even when there is a crisis or a stressful deadline, we do not revert back to fear and control. We can instead fall back on the trust we have built with colleagues.

5. The organization is equitable, generative, and fair.

Non-hierarchical organizations are challenged to have a more meaningful purpose and more equitable ways—whether in their salaries, profit sharing, environmental impact, or getting along with others despite differences. These ways are a deliberate step away from extractive, coercive, patriarchal ways. Those are strong words, but they do reflect the paradigms from which our current top-down organizational frameworks and culture have grown. The only way an organization can be fully horizontal is if the organization has meaning for its workers. Then it can easily relinquish control and allow people to own their personal leadership and contribute to the organization.

Getting Unstuck When Going Horizontal

How can you bring about this new way of being without getting frustrated and overwhelmed or without having everything backfire? Moving from aspiration to action is not easy. We carry within us a load of assumptions that support top-down ways and hold us back from developing new behaviors. We are hoping for some easy instruction guide or recipe book, but we know that each organization has its own path to self-management. Some are coming to horizontal ways accidentally, some intentionally, and some begrudgingly. The transition sounds exhausting. Despite genuine and growing interest in more horizontal ways of working, organizations are getting stuck in making the transition.

Here's an example. A Canadian bank sets up a new initiative: management invites employees who see a process or way of working that doesn't make sense to bring it forward so it can be changed. This initiative sounds great, and the intention is good, but what are the chances it will get stuck? Employees put their requests in the hands of management, who have decision-making and action-taking power—it's the parent-to-child culture at play. If an idea doesn't get enacted, not only will there be no change, but employees will become less engaged, not more. Fully stepping into an adult-to-adult partnership culture is necessary for such a change in process to flourish. Short of working on these fundamental shifts, most change processes will stall.

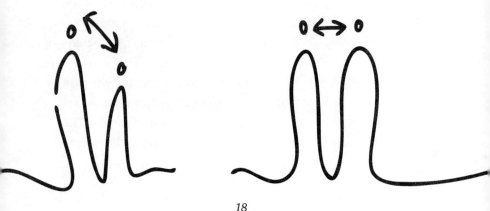

Most people think that when they change to a new system, they need to be good at it from the get-go and have figured out all the details of the journey. The shift is projected to be huge and comprehensive, and this is overwhelming. People also assume that they need to start a revolution with full buy-in from organizational leaders before they are able to do anything. It is no wonder most organizations get stuck!

DON'T DO IT ALL AT ONCE

Whatever happened to just trying things out and learning from them? That is how we all learned to walk and talk. If we are changing to a new system, we need to give ourselves space for errors and learning. Otherwise, what you get is only fair-weather projects. That is, as soon as a situation or challenge arises, and invariably one will, we scapegoat the self-managing initiative and return to conventional ways. We might even go so far as to call it "dogmatic" or "risky" or "inefficient," as though conventional methods are free from dogma, risk, and inefficiency! All the terms we can come up with are shields we build to protect us from changing the paradigm. The reality is that all of us need to learn these horizontal ways and bring them into play within our specific work contexts and domains.

Most organizations have been set up with the goal of making them well-tuned machines that allow them to plan and control into a predictable future. This mind-set is what we call "mechanistic," and it involves employees working individually and in highly specialized roles. Humans in these systems have internalized mechanistic reflexes, and shifting into a horizontal mind-set requires adopting a "living-systems" way of thinking.

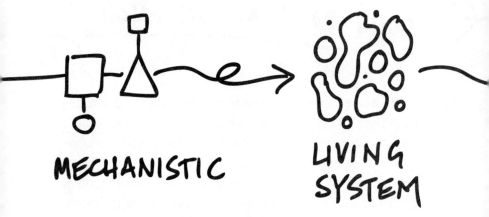

MECHANISTIC   LIVING SYSTEM

Living-systems organizations are like a city where things are in constant flux, ever responding to changes within and around them. Of course, even if we understand and accept this principle, that does not mean that we are able to operationalize it on a daily basis within our work world. The assumptions and structures of most organizations invite us to do just the opposite. There is no magic wand for going horizontal, and there will be bumps in the road. The path forward is through practice.

TWO

PRACTICING IS THE PATH TO MASTERY

But I don't want to go into the water;
I only want to learn how to swim.

Develop a Horizontal Mind-Set through Practice, Now

Going horizontal is *not* about flipping a switch. It is a deeper, internal shift, with new behaviors and reflexes. This can take time to develop, and anyone can strengthen and grow their non-hierarchical mind-set at any time. What do I mean when I say horizontal ways are a "practice"? Practice means the learning requires constant repetition. It is doing the same thing over and over, adjusting and tweaking each time. It is a learning-in-action process.

Some people think they need to have the buy-in of their organizational decision makers to be able to start implementing non-hierarchical ways. Incorrect! Here are four reasons to start developing this horizontal mind-set through non-hierarchical practices now:

1. **The whole idea of non-hierarchical ways is to own your personal leadership.** Therefore, we cannot just wait for the hierarchy to usher it in. If horizontal ways are important to us, then it is time to pull up our sleeves and step into action. We cannot wait for the hierarchy to initiate a shift to non-hierarchy.

2. **Much of the work of shifting to a non-hierarchical mind-set is internal.** Hence, anyone can begin at any time. In fact, the person who stands to benefit the most by engaging in these horizontal practices is you. It is really about becoming aware of the habits and reflexes that you carry within yourself from hierarchical command and control culture and replacing them with new habits and reflexes. Not only do the practices help all of us become better workers, but they help us become better humans (partners, parents, friends, citizens).

3. **You don't really know the future.** Your organization and your place of work might change in ways that you can't foresee. If you start horizontal practices, you can never really know how the ripples will affect those around you. You can invest in expanding your range of ways of being with other people and doing work without being attached to where it will go. When a time comes that your organization shifts to more horizontal ways, your awareness and skills in the new habits will be a gift and an advantage.

..... future ...

4. **Sometimes people focus on non-hierarchical structural and policy shifts that have more immediate visibility.** These shifts are important, don't get me wrong, but without non-hierarchical practices in place they will flounder. Structures alone do not mean that people will reconnect with their natural self-organizing instincts to function with trust, mutual care, and initiative taking. Practices help navigate the deep cultural shift.

PRACTICE

What Defines a Practice?

Practice, that is, doing something over and over and over to facilitate mastery, is perfectly natural for humans in every culture. Through practice we learn to speak a language, drive a car, play an instrument, hunt for quarry, cook a meal, converse with others. You name the skill, we all know that if we give time to deliberate practice, we get better at it. With a martial art, for example, we do the moves over and over to strengthen the muscles, create new automatic reflexes within us, feel when the moves are right and when they are aligned. We practice together to get the feedback offered by the presence of others. We can both challenge and support one another in our practices.

Practice does not by any means take the form of a free-for-all. We get masterful at performing judo not just by putting in hundreds of random hours but by giving ourselves methods and frameworks, and by reflecting on how well we are doing, what is holding us back, and where we want to grow.

This self-reflection invites a deeper analysis of our personal assumptions and beliefs that might need to shift. Whenever I refer to the term *practice*, I am including these three components: (1) the actual doing, (2) some principles or processes that provide a minimal structure to hold the practice, and (3) self-reflection. For example in soccer, the actual doing means that you are playing soccer rather than talking about playing soccer. A practice structure could

be taking 20 penalty shots in a row where you focus on hitting different precise spots in the goal. Self-reflection could be analyzing from the 20 penalty shots where your strengths and weaknesses lie to give yourself further targeted practice. This sequence is sometimes referred to as a do–observe–reflect loop to help shift and grow new habits and skills. Practices don't happen by osmosis. We need to intentionally and actively initiate new behaviors.

Somewhere the notion of practice got mixed up with the notion of expertise. Thinking in terms of expertise can make us feel incompetent or no longer in need of more learning. By contrast, practice accepts us exactly where we are. Practice is kind. Practice invites us into our doubt and discomfort, into the messy imperfection so we can grow. Practice says just try; that's how we learn. It's a never-ending path of doing, tweaking, and doing again.

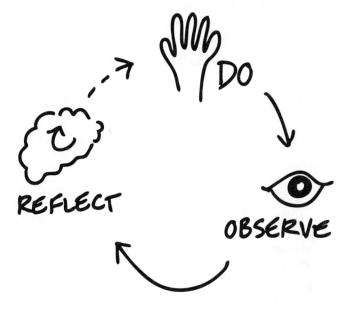

Three Types of Practice

The practices in this book fall into three categories or types. I have created the categories as a way to help you be more conscious and strategic with your practices. Note that it is important that you find spaces to practice that have psychological safety and where you will not risk your job or your professional reputation. Intentionally choosing which type of practice is appropriate for any given situation will help you grow your horizontal culture one step at a time, and help you avoid getting stuck.

I.   **Personal practices.** Personal practices don't require any formal permission or agreement with others to try out. They are individual practices that might not even be noticed by others, while still holding power and potential for transformation. They have a power to model a way forward for oneself and others. The practitioner benefits enormously by implementing a personal practice because these practices help us with our inner work. They help us be more self-aware about subtleties. Personal practices can be done internally anywhere, no matter what the external context is. They can benefit us in all aspects of our lives, in work and beyond work. Examples might be asking for help, listening in a deep way, and getting grounded.

2. **Safe practices.** Some practices require the involvement and consent of other people; they have a collective element to them. Safe practices are those where we can engage these exterior forces in contexts that offer care and kindness for us. These are practices we do with colleagues whom we trust. They allow us to flex our muscles on practices outside of the work world, with friends or in our community groups and clubs. With a bit of practice, they can be brought to the next level. Examples might be collective decision making, collective sensemaking, and team meeting practices.

3. **Trial practices.** Trial practices are those that can be proposed to a group. It is important that they be proposed as prototypes. That is, try them multiple times in order to gather learnings and insights about how to work better together. These are the practices that can help shift an entire organizational culture and structure.

I highly suggest that you begin with the first two practice types before stepping into the third. In the beginning you will have enough work to do to shed a hierarchical mind-set and step more fully into a non-hierarchical mind-set.

Practices Are for Everyone, No Matter Your Role

The seven domains of practices we delve into in this book are pervasive across all organizations. They all begin at an individual level, and they grow from there. They help us show up differently in our organizations, but they are nothing strange or foreign. On the contrary, these are ways that are deeply familiar to us because we already practice them in our personal lives. We are just bringing them into our work worlds, with adjustments for the context of work. These are the practices:

1. **Autonomy:** Figuring out what we want to be doing or need to be doing

2. **Purpose:** Keeping purpose rather than our egos at the heart of what we're doing

3. **Meetings:** Conducting our meetings collaboratively

4. **Transparency:** Sharing with one another and trusting one another

5. **Decision Making:** Making decisions where others' voices are heard and action is the focus

6. **Learning and Development:** Growing and developing ourselves beyond our current assumptions and limitations

7. **Relationships and Conflicts:** Nurturing relationships with our fellow human beings

With repetition self-organization will begin to feel like the normal and healthy way for an organization to function.

We All Start in Different Places

If you are a manager, your challenge might be to create spaces to allow others to initiate their personal leadership. You have influence, sometimes more than you realize. If people are accustomed to you calling the shots, you will need to create the void that others can occupy and support others who are activating their personal leadership. A question to keep in mind is "How can my vision, skills, and strategy be leveraged for the organization while inviting others into theirs?" As a manager you might also be in a position to protect a space for those below you to experiment with non-hierarchical practices.

If you are not in a management position, your challenge might be in stepping up. You might be accustomed to waiting for others to act on your behalf, whereas there are in fact many small practices that you can enter into that can grow horizontal ways. Taking up these practices will require stepping out of your comfort zone: speaking up, making proposals, taking action where you are. You will need to navigate the power structures of your organization with care and courage, and sometimes you will need to assess when it is time to let go as well. You will be in a completely different frame of mind when you are in a non-hierarchical mind-set. It means that if you notice something that needs to be done, you figure out an action or proposal to move it forward or you let it go. You will begin to become aware of the permission culture that's part of your mind-set, and you will step away from that and further into your personal leadership.

Straddling Two Paradigms

Each and every one of us is probably already engaged in various non-hierarchical practices within our families and communities as well as our work worlds without even realizing it. After all, self-organization is part of human nature. Much of what you will discover in this book will feel familiar because we are just bringing these normal ways of being into our work worlds (with adjustment for the context of work). These are practices that have gotten a little lost in the organizational culture and structures that we have created for ourselves, but they are practices that we can rekindle and grow while we continue to do business. It is a bit like building a bicycle as we cycle on it, so it will be a bit messy, and that is okay!

You will likely find yourself in situations where you need to straddle both vertical and horizontal practices for a while. Your two worlds are co-existing. Breathe and accept it. A fundamental shift like this requires a foot in two worlds.

By taking up non-hierarchical practices at work, you will be able to see and acknowledge them elsewhere in your life and grow them further. You might notice non-hierarchical ways being used in a professional community or an informal group you are part of. One practice space can feed another. Since you expect and desire non-hierarchical ways in the informal spaces in your life, your non-hierarchical practice can grow there too.[11] As you begin to bring a horizontal lens to the different situations in your life, your opportunities for practice will grow. The more your personal practices strengthen and grow, the more you will feel able to propose practices to others in your workplace. Then you will begin connecting with existing practices around you and helping expand them. Like a plant that receives water and sunlight, the practices will grow and grow. Slowly but surely, successful horizontal practices will shine the way to your organization's future.

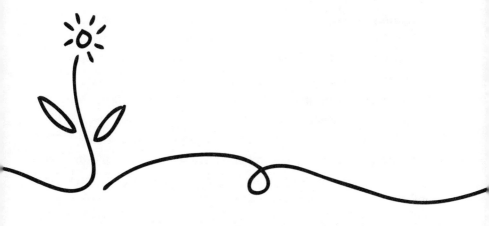

THREE

AUTONOMY

Claim Your Personal Leadership

Control leads to compliance, autonomy to engagement.
Daniel Pink

Why Autonomy Is Important

Autonomy is the capacity to manage one's own time within a domain of constraints. It is not unbridled freedom. Trust, specifically trusting people to manage themselves, with the interest both of others and the organization in mind, is the foundation of a horizontal culture. In fact, it is difficult to claim that employees are trusted at all if they are not allowed to make decisions about their own time and workflows. Most people don't like to be controlled. They want to be able to make their own choices at work. In a horizontal culture, this ability is an operational necessity.

Workplace performance is linked to employee trust. Workplace autonomy fosters enthusiasm and innovation. People feel valued as intelligent human beings. People wither and disengage under micromanagement, whereas they thrive and engage when they are treated as competent and capable adults.[12] If you want your colleagues to engage with their work but also to make decisions and take responsibility with the well-being of the company in mind, you will find that autonomy will grow that mind-set. People will rise up to become the contributors they are expected to be. You might be fearful that people will not do their work, will take advantage of the organization, or put the organization at risk. However, experience tells us the opposite. Relinquishing control unleashes human potential and creativity.

Owners of medium businesses who have had to absent themselves from the workplace for periods of time are surprised to discover that in their absence, employees are able to get on with things without being controlled.[13] Autonomy also increases a business's ability to attract and retain employees. Autonomy is a critical factor for employee well-being. But how do we create autonomy? What are some low-risk ways we can let go of control? What are the practices that can be developed to help maintain or increase performance with autonomy? In this chapter we explore four ways to practice autonomy: (1) self-managing where and when we work, (2) self-organizing of our tasks, (3) taking responsibility and dealing with difficult situations, and (4) giving more flexibility in roles and accountability. To fully embrace autonomy requires new organizational policies. This chapter helps you understand the range of autonomy possible, the practices that support autonomy, and how you might take autonomy to the next level in your organization. That can mean making small proposals or experiments, slowly increasing autonomy without having to upend the whole system.

Humans Are Wired for Autonomous Behavior

As human beings we function autonomously. Each and every day we do chores like taking out the garbage, bringing home the groceries, or paying the bills.

We are just plain good at autonomy. We plan vacations and renovate our homes. We manage where we need to be, what we want to do, where our priorities lie, how we collaborate with others, and how we manage our time. We accomplish these things without anybody overseeing us, and we bear the consequences of our actions.

Sometimes requests are tossed back and forth as responsibility is divvied up between partners or friends. Hey, I made dinner, will you do the dishes? This is not a hierarchical dynamic. The art of successful personal dynamics, adult to adult, is one where there is no authority or hierarchy. A healthy functional relationship between friends or a couple should accomplish things without either individual feeling managed by the other. We never want to feel like the other party is trying to control us. Even children take offense when adults try to curb their autonomy. Autonomy is truly a core value and practice in our personal lives.

Self-Managing When and Where You Work

Today's work world is changing rapidly. Technology is enabling productivity to thrive with an unprecedented amount of flexibility. Expectations with regard to where and when people work are changing too. Given this changing landscape, autonomy in location and schedule are a good place to start with the horizontal practice of autonomy. To be clear, autonomy in location and schedule does *not* simply mean that everyone works when and where they want. Organizational constraints should determine what the autonomy will look like in each individual situation. It does mean that an authority figure should not determine when and where everyone should work. Workers should create and evolve a system among themselves that makes sense for the organization and themselves. Like everything else in a horizontal workplace, in order to succeed, an organization must have a system of practices that underpin the structure.

Guiding Principles

How do you ensure professional behavior within autonomy? I could rephrase that and say, "How can you trust your colleagues?" Here are three practices to help:

1. **The organization comes first.** When there is a conflict between personal preference and what is best for the organization, the organization's needs should always be paramount. For example, if someone is a night owl this does not give them leave to miss a project meeting that starts at 9 a.m. Team members are expected to fully participate in structures that are best for the team, even when they might prefer a different time.

2. **Acknowledge challenging habits.** In order for autonomy to work, everyone must regulate their own behavior. For example, the draw of social media is strong, but team members need to acknowledge this and make personal commitments to check it only a few times a day. Having group agreements and co-created policies regarding these common challenges can help.

3. **State your limits.** Clearly stated boundaries are critical to the success of autonomy. For example, to protect your personal space, communicate clear parameters around what can be expected of you in the evenings and on weekends. If one member of a team prefers to work on weekends but the rest of the team does not, the team cannot be expected to respond to requests for a quick turnaround on weekends.

The more autonomy an organization allows, the more responsibility falls on workers to think about how they need to function in order to meet the needs of the organization and stay true to their personal productivity profiles.

When You Work

Some industries have more time and space constraints than others. The retail industry must be staffed during the hours that the store is open, whereas a factory must be staffed to optimize the machinery, often with 24-hour shift work. Practices of self-managing workplace and time can be tailored for all work contexts. The defining feature of a horizontal organization is that the workers are the ones who establish the tracking system. For example, some factories in Mondragon, Spain, have functioned for decades with workers establishing their own work schedules and tracking their hours.[14] Where I worked 20 years ago as a professional in the public sector, employees tracked their own time on a private spreadsheet. We established the following rules with our boss: The work week is 40 hours (on average) and the work day occurs between 7 a.m. and 6 p.m. If you see that you are accumulating overtime hours, then you need to proactively check in with the director to talk this through and find an agreement.

At the company where I work today, Percolab, there is no tracking whatsoever of when we work. We are free to work the hours we want. This level of autonomy allows people who are high performing in the evening as well as the morning to unleash their full potential. We all show up at team meetings and for shared project work, but outside of that, the night owls can work the hours when they can be most productive. We are happy to be able to be on the same team in this way. However, in other organizational contexts this level of autonomy is not appropriate. It's all about matching your level of autonomy to the context.

> List the parameters at your organization around when you work. Do you have the amount of autonomy you wish for in when you work? Do your colleagues? Based on the three principles above, what could you do to increase your practice of autonomy?

Where You Work

Autonomy in where you work requires a certain vision from your organization because it is entwined with organizational policies and workplace design. This aspect of autonomy cannot, of course, be managed on the individual level but can come into play when an organization is seeking to integrate more autonomy and horizontal practices into its culture. Two ways an organization can increase autonomy in where you work are office design and organizational policies.

More and more, office redesigns are creating multifunctional spaces that afford people more options in where they work. These spaces make possible increased autonomy on the premises of the organization.

Policies that allow employees to work outside the office can also result in mutually beneficial arrangements. For some this starts with permission to work from home. Giving employees the option to work from home on specific days has been shown to have all sorts of benefits for organizations, from increased productivity to increased loyalty.[15] Some offices are removing all restrictions. For example, one division of 60 people at an intergovernmental European agency gives employees freedom regarding where and when they work.[16] Employees focus on being available for team meetings and achieving deliverables. This simple guideline has injected a huge amount of autonomy within the unit, which has no trouble attracting talent. And at Percolab, we all agree to be physically in the office an average of two days a week and attend at least 70 percent of weekly team meetings (physically or virtually) and read all meeting notes for those meetings we miss.

Having autonomy in when and where we work requires new personal management practices. Some people work too much, starting earlier and finishing later; they are not used to all that extra time created once they are freed from commuting and feel guilty about the privilege. These people will need to figure out ways to give themselves a proper break, such as putting on a timer or being intentional about going for a walk. Of course, some people will be tempted to let accountability slide, so it is important to discuss self-accountability measures as well. You might want to create new gestures such as sending a morning chat to your team to let them know you are "in the office" or requiring that your online availability status is always accurate and states clearly whether you are available or not. Acknowledging that these practices are important and swapping strategies with colleagues can also be helpful.

No matter where you work, identify something that you can do differently with regard to where you work or where you take your break. If possible, try a walk-and-talk meeting outside and see how that feels.

Is there something specific you would like to change in your organization's policies about when and where you work? If so, make a plan to move that change forward.

Self-Organizing Tasks—The Kanban Board

If we can figure out which tasks to do and how to prioritize them in our personal lives, we can surely do that in our work lives. The technology sector has made great headway in this area with what has become known as the "agile movement." It is built on the premise that with a clear goal and an incremental approach to project management, individuals are perfectly capable of self-organizing their tasks. Though the agile movement was developed within the tech sector, many of its practices are easily transposable to other sectors. One practice is to self-assign tasks using a shared visual tool—one very useful method is called a kanban board. I outline the basic structure of a kanban board method here, but further reading will give you a myriad of different ways to implement this valuable tool.

To begin, list all the work that you want to accomplish for a specific project within a specific period. Keep the periods to a manageable duration, a matter of weeks, in order to prevent burnout and task overload. Once this list has been created, create a three-column chart—in any medium from a physi-

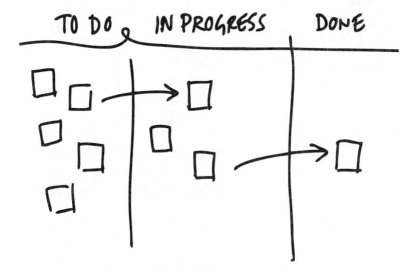

cal poster to a spreadsheet to a kanban app. Label the three columns "To Do," "In Progress," and "Done." When you are ready to work on a task, move it out of the To Do space and into the In Progress space, and when it is finished, move it to the Done space. You will experience a sense of accomplishment when you move it to the Done space.

If you were to bring this method of working with tasks into a group, the critical element that changes everything is to make sure you assign tasks only to yourself and that you move only your own task. It might try your patience, but it is important to rewire this reflex. This does not mean you shouldn't invite people to do a task, or let everyone know how an unassigned or incomplete task is interconnected with your task. What you want is for the term *delegate* to drop away as people learn to self-delegate their own tasks. As the task proceeds through its different phases, the task owner moves it across the board.

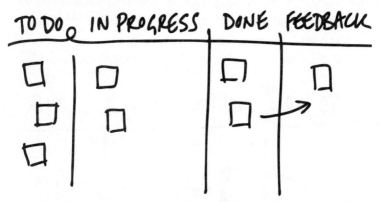

The basic structure of this technique can be expanded. For example, you could add a "Feedback" or "Validation" column to the end. Then—again with each person moving only their own tasks—team members can put tasks that they are explicitly requesting feedback or validation on in this column to solicit input. In this way colleagues have an instant view where they can offer feedback or validation to keep things moving.

Regular "stand-up meetings"— brief moments when everyone checks in (standing up) to state what they have worked on or are currently working on and any blockages or requests for help—are part of this practice, whether held once a week or every day.

Further reading about kanban boards can help you find many examples of ways that people set them up and the types of online systems that support self-organizing tasks for distributed teams. This practice will require buy-in of your team members, and possibly managerial support if you are still working in a more vertical organization. However, if you can propose it as a trial, it will still contribute to a horizontal mind-set, even if done by a work team within a larger vertical organization.

When we first tried this at Percolab, I almost had to sit on my hands to stop myself from moving others' cards from one column to another. Moving others' cards would hinder the development of autonomy. If we want to support the development of personal leadership of our colleagues, we need to let go of telling them what to do. This is true for everyone, and for managers even more so.

When I brought the kanban board method to the Montreal Urban Ecology Centre, the only place to put the board was in the big stairwell leading from the reception area up to the offices. Years have gone by, the staff has changed, but this self-organization practice remains, with the big board still in the stairwell. The practice is amazingly efficient and makes it easier to ask for and offer help, and this functionality has resulted in the practice enduring despite a change of management.

You can make use of kanban boards, individually or in a group, in a wide variety of ways. For example, they can be used to manage business leads and administration of contracts.

The column headings can be whatever you need according to your context.

LEADS	QUOTES	CONTRACTS	PROJECTS IN PROGRESS	CLOSING
☐	☐	☐	☐	☐
☐	☐		☐	
			☐	
			☐	

What makes this practice work is the fact that the objective or goal is clear for everyone to see. That goal serves as a guide, enabling everyone to see the status of the whole project by looking at others' cards on the board. But remember, this practice is as much about knowing what tasks you want to take on as it is about not intervening and telling others what they should be doing!

Identify something that you usually delegate to your colleagues. How would you feel if you let them decide for themselves about this work?

Taking Responsibility

We know that autonomy is about having the freedom to choose within a realm of constraints and general direction, but there is no autonomy without responsibility. The two go hand in hand. The question that makes people nervous about relinquishing control and allowing autonomy to flourish is "But will they be able to assume responsibility?" In the vertical paradigm, management is constantly putting up checkpoints for performance to ensure that people are taking responsibility. What happens when we are no longer looking to our manager for this but are accountable to our colleagues? If practiced well, responsibility and accountability are much stronger in a horizontal culture than in a vertical culture; if practiced poorly, though, they will be weaker than in a conventional organization.

Taking Responsibility for What You Notice

Here is a practice you can do that will help you see yourself as an active agent within the organization. If you are not working in a horizontal organization, you will first need to delineate the actual zone of influence that you have: it might be tiny, and that is fine. For example, if you are involved in the management of the office fridge, you can change how it is maintained, or if you take part in organizational meetings, you can influence how they take place.

It is important to become self-aware of automatic reflexes when there is a situation that needs to be improved within your zone of influence. A typical vertical reflex is to become frustrated with the situation, disassociate from it, and focus on personal desires. A typical horizontal reflex begins with inquiry to better understand the situation. For example, if you are frustrated with the meeting culture in your organization, start here: "Why are meetings run in this way? How long have meetings been run like this?" Then you can begin to see yourself as a contributor to the solution. "Is there something I could do to help improve our meetings? Is there something I want to try out?" When you approach a situation from this perspective, you have made it a collective process, shown respect for the stake your colleagues have in that situation, and positioned yourself in such a way as to contribute to a collective solution. You take responsibility when you take ownership of the situation. You see yourself as part of the situation because you have built the authority to move it forward. That can sound like "Does anyone want to help me craft a proposal to improve the way meetings function?"

To summarize, to see yourself as an active agent in the organization,

- Engage in *inquiry* about the situation. Try to understand why things are like this.

- See yourself as *contributing* to improving the situation while seeing the situation as owned by others.

- Take *ownership* of the situation and agency in changing it. After engaging in inquiry, you will have a better understanding of the situation. You can then say, "I have

a proposal to improve the way our meetings are run. The reason I am making this proposal is..."

The reality is that if you are not working in a fully horizontal organization, some situations are outside your realm of influence. For these you can either find a way to make peace within yourself about the situation or move on from the organization.

Identify three situations within your area of work. It doesn't matter how small they are (in fact, it can be helpful to start with small ones). For each situation identify which type of responsibility thought patterns you are experiencing using the list above (inquiry, contributing, ownership, or frustration). What do you notice?

Finding Clarity

A second practice of taking responsibility is to actively develop clarity about what you should be doing and how best to do it. In vertical culture a manager determines these things and hands them down to the employees, but in a horizontal culture you need new reflexes. When you're faced with the question "What should I do?" here are three questions that can help you achieve clarity in your priorities:

1. Refer to the purpose of the organization, the project, the role. Looking at the big picture or desired outcome will serve as a guiding light and help you avoid the pitfall of losing track of what's important.

2. Speak to someone who has some experience in the area of your proposal. A horizontal culture does not mean that you disregard experience and expertise. Seek it out and invite it in. You should seek out excellence. The expertise might be internal to your organization, but it might also be external.

3. Speak to someone who might be the audience or user. By doing so, you bring in the wisdom and perspective of those on the receiving end of your proposal.

These questions are enough to replace the conventional vertical communication channel. If you work in a vertical organization where you need to report to a manager, you can still engage in this practice; when you meet with that person, include your conclusions in discussions.

The personal practices of taking responsibility and finding clarity are the most subtle and difficult practices to develop and the most critical in a horizontal mind-set. In order to enter into an adult-to-adult partnership culture, you need to increase the awareness of your thought patterns and behaviors that perpetuate a child-to-adult dynamic. You can't have successful autonomy without developing these reflexes.

> Identify a specific recent occasion when you went to your boss for clarification and guidance. Based on the three alternative reflexes above, what might you have done instead?

Exchanging Job Descriptions for Roles

Job descriptions are a deeply entrenched policy in organizations. Dealing with them can breed frustration: some people don't like being asked to do things outside their job descriptions while others are frustrated that they need permission to take on something outside of them. But an organization can let go of the conventional notion of attributing a job description to individuals. Indeed, for organizations in domains of work that are subject to change, prescriptive job descriptions can even compromise a capacity for responsiveness. The team or organization can distribute work in ways that support responsiveness and flexibility: they can organize based on "roles." For example, at my company we have a role called "first respondent." This role is accountable for handling all the requests we receive through our company email. Since the purpose, accountabilities, and associated processes are so clearly and simply documented, this role can be easily passed among employees. Here are three practices that enable a successful role-based structure:

1. Having self-awareness of what is right for you to be doing

2. Shifting from ownership to stewardship

3. Holding one another accountable

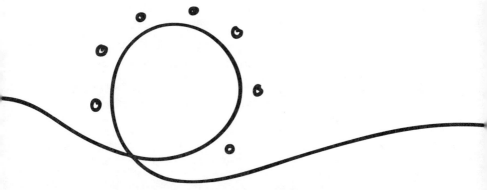

Having Self-Awareness of What Roles to Take On

When an organization shifts to roles, it invites individuals to increase their self-awareness of what they should be doing. For example, an organization I worked for in the past shifted from a structure of *titles* (project manager, coordinator, etc.) to one of *project roles*: the *operational role* gets the work done and handles problematic issues; the *strategic role* ensures accountability and a focus on a wider view, making sure the project fits into the overall organizational strategy; and the *administrative* role deals with contractual and partnership issues. Different people in the organization could therefore take care of different roles on different projects. In adopting this structure, the organization gained a new level of modularity and flexibility. The fact that each role was documented in detail and approved by everyone added to organizational clarity. From there everyone developed their own self-awareness of what they should be focusing on.

Here are three tensions you need to navigate:

1. What you have the energy to do versus what needs to be done

2. Your strengths versus your desire to learn something new

3. What you should be doing versus what others should be doing

Roles can be set up in many different ways, and the structure should be determined by the specific needs of your organization. Generally, a thriving horizontal organization will have both universal roles (those held by everyone in the organization simultaneously) and more targeted, individual roles.

Here is an example of what a role can look like at Percolab:

Working Tools Mechanic

- Support the team to be in flow and ease to work remotely (with help from IT experts)
- team has appropriate access to applications and this is documented
- team feels at ease with their tools
- support is given for decision making processes on new tools
- create and maintain guidelines for usage.

Indicator of role well stewarded: No incidents from team not being in sync

If you want more extensive guidance on a fully role-based system, the Holacracy approach is helpful.[17] No matter the system, you will be continually confronted with the three tensions.

> Think of something you have been wanting to do in your organization. Think about that thing in the context of the three tensions: energy versus need; strengths versus learning; you versus others. Does anything become clear?

Stewardship versus Ownership

Roles belong not to a person but to the organization. It can take a while to deconstruct ownership reflexes. For many people, identity gets entangled with work. For some tasks, it can feel disconcerting if a role or task is passed on to someone else. What will I be without this role? To clarify, a role can't be owned by anyone, but that doesn't mean that everyone has to be able to do every role. If you find yourself referring to a role as "my role," that is a semantic indicator that you might still be in the ownership paradigm. For this reason, strong formal guidelines might be needed to help develop our new habits. Here is one approach, inspired from Holacracy:

- Anyone can modify the content of any existing role, create a new role, or retire a role. This needs to be collectively agreed upon in order to take effect.

- Everyone ensures that all roles are being stewarded well. Each individual is considered responsible for making sure all roles are attended to. While all roles may not be active at all times, the collective organization still has the responsibility to make sure that each role is claimed when it is needed.

- At any time, anyone can relinquish a role. Role rotation meetings should be a regular and scheduled element when this structure is used.

- An individual who stewards a role drives the necessary processes to ensure that the role achieves its potential and purpose. These processes include identifying next actions, defining projects, ensuring their movement, and keeping others informed.

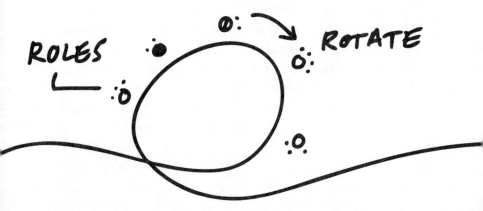

Holding One Another Accountable

Management is about holding ourselves and others account-able. With a well-written role, everyone should understand the importance of the role and the impact on the organization if it is poorly carried out. Ideally, a role has one or two met-rics of accountability embedded in it. You likely have a sense when a role is not being well carried out. What do you do if the responsible person is someone you like or if the intentions are good? If you have a horizontal mind-set, you must look at the well-being of the organization. It is not only acceptable but even essential to speak up to let everyone know that there is a problem with the role. By speaking up, you allow the or-ganization to look at solutions together. Holding one another accountable might not be easy, but it is the responsible thing to do. Here are three things to keep your focus on:

1. The impact of the role and evaluation metrics for it

2. The accountability of the role and not the person responsible for it

3. Ways to improve the role through constructive comments and ideas (rather than by blaming)

If you still function with a job description, pick two func-tions from it. Identify the purpose of these functions and why each is important.

How would you feel if someone else was accountable for them for a while?

Summary

This chapter focuses on four key practices that can help develop individual and collective capacity for autonomy.

1. **Self-manage when and where you work.** Make sure the organization comes first, work on your challenging habits, and make your limits known. These practices involve tracking time and space constraints, being intentional, and developing self-awareness of your productivity rhythms and needs.

2. **Self-organize your tasks (and resist delegating).** Use tools, such as the kanban board, to facilitate working with others without delegating. The kanban board creates conditions that foster workers' support of one another. It does require that you acknowledge your reflex when you want to control how someone does something.

3. **Take responsibility for situations.** Make the inner shift of taking responsibility and developing your reflex to actively address situations that arise around you. Gain clarity about the situation by consulting purpose, experts, and users.

4. **Organize around roles and hold one another accountable.** Go beyond job descriptions and develop self-awareness in what you should be doing for the organization through roles. See yourself as a steward on behalf of the organization rather than taking ownership of an area of work.

Autonomy is achievable when individuals keep their focus on the organization. Then increased trust and freedom can flow.

FOUR

PURPOSE

The Invisible Leader

If you want to build a ship, don't drum up the people to
gather wood, divide the work, and give orders. Instead,
teach them to yearn for the vast and endless sea.
Antoine de Saint-Exupéry

Why Purpose Is Important

Non-hierarchical work culture is not everyone going off in
their own direction. It is quite the opposite; it's a way of
working together in service of the organization's purpose.
Everyone looks to purpose as the invisible leader. Everyone
treats purpose not just as a catchy phrase written on the
wall but as the beacon around which everything can ar-
ticulate and come together. Once an organization (and its
managers) releases control to a wider group, the only way
that group can successfully function with a high dose of
autonomy and alignment is if the organizational purpose
is crystal clear. It doesn't need to micromanage, and an

adult-to-adult partnership culture can grow. Once the why is clear, people can figure out the how. They can figure out if an idea might have value for the organization: if, for example, it makes sense to take on a specific contract, or if a policy needs adjusting. People can check in on purpose to figure things out together.

Purpose is important not just at the organizational level but everywhere. Whenever we ask, "What's the objective here?" we are checking in with purpose, whether it is the purpose of a new product, a job profile, or a report. Almost everything we do in an organization has a purpose: for example, the financial dashboard keeps the organization on track, and a team dinner celebrates completing a project on time. In a horizontal culture, purpose is everyone's business. Instead of cleaning your desk so you don't get into trouble, you do it because you want to contribute to the collective ambience of the office. Not only those with higher rank determine and drive purpose. Everyone shares a collective responsibility to make purpose explicit, to keep it on track and up to date. You can forget about blindly following rules and procedures, tasks and orders, and connect with the why behind things. Purpose is less a goal than an essential practice that drives non-hierarchical ways.

In this chapter we look at four practices of purpose: (1) clarifying purpose, (2) using purpose to support inviting rather than obliging, (3) taking responsibility for purpose, and (4) aligning with purpose.

We Naturally Check In with
Purpose All the Time

"What was the purpose of your trip?" "Business, education, work, pleasure" are the options on the customs card you have to fill out.

```
PURPOSE    ☐ BUSINESS      ☑ WORK
OF TRIP?   ☐ EDUCATION     ☐ PLEASURE
```

We check in with purpose all the time without even thinking about it. Imagine that you want to rent a new apartment. You would rent a very different place depending on whether your purpose is to prepare for a baby or reconnect with yourself after a breakup. Purpose guides our actions and decisions. If I had a skillful bartender, I could order a drink based on purpose: "I want a drink that relaxes me." You are not telling the bartender with any precision what you want; the purpose is enough. We know how to separate the why from the how. If my intention is to clear my mind, I have options: I can go to the gym, take a bath, go shopping. If I commit to running a marathon, my purpose will sustain me and energize me in my moments of doubt and help me make it through. If I have dinner with a friend, I intuitively know that the reason we meet is to share company and tell stories together.

In our personal lives, purpose is so integrated, we are not always conscious of the many ways it influences our actions.

Clarifying Purpose

Purpose is the intention we put into the things we do. It is the why that underlies everything, including where we sit at work, how we organize our documents, when we take our vacations, and the way we speak to our colleagues. We don't necessarily bother ourselves with thinking about it all the time, as that can be exhausting. However, when the purpose is not clear, we can get confused. For example, if we need to produce a report, some might think the report serves to document a process, others might think it is about stating recommendations going forward, and still others might understand it as a way to build trust. Here are three ways you can clarify purpose when you see that the purpose is not clear. These tactics can be used individually or collectively, and they can apply to anything from a company-wide project to attending a conference to writing a report.

1. Stop and Listen.

Sometimes in the flow of day-to-day business, you lose track of what the purpose is. When you notice that you are confused, stop and listen. What is your purpose here? The time you take doesn't need to be long. A bit of spaciousness and silence can help to reveal it. Sometimes that is all that is required. Imagine that you want to help someone fine-tune their questions on their course of action. Rather than jumping in with techniques and methods, you might want to ask, "What are we trying to do by fine-tuning the questions?" or "Why is it important to fine-tune questions?" Then you would remember that it's about helping the person have clarity on their line of inquiry. Without that clarity you could waste energy going in the wrong direction.

2. Connect to Inspiration.

It can often be helpful to connect with purpose on an inspirational level. You want any purpose to speak to you clearly and simply. This process can be used to help clarify the purpose of a task, a project, or an organization, as well as in many other contexts. Here are five ways to use inspiration to get to purpose:

- Think of an anecdote that communicates strong and meaningful purpose.
- How you felt when you first connected with this task/project/organization?
- What do you love about this task/project/ organization?
- What is a potential that you sense in this task/ project/organization?
- What is an impact you deeply desire for this task/project/organization?

Once something comes to you, you can write down a purpose with the first thing that comes to mind, no overthinking. Usually that will be an inspired purpose. If you do this with a group and share, taking a moment to soak in what everyone has come up with and letting go of a desire for things to be formulated this way or that, energy and direction often bubble up and become crystal clear.

3. Go to the Source.

The essence of purpose lies at the impulse of creation. When a project, or a new policy or process or product, is brought into being, that birthing moment is usually a moment where the purpose is alive and clear. To get clarity on purpose, you can often go back to the source.

Identify some situation in your organization that lacks clarity in purpose. Choose one of the three approaches above and clarify the purpose.

Inviting Rather Than Obliging

Most people like to be invited to do something rather than required to do something. Organizations tend to forget this, but in a horizontal culture, inviting people is foundational. When you invite people, you move away from "Do this because you have to" and move toward "I invite you to do this because we are here and this is where we are going and I have some clarity on a good way for us to get there." Speaking to the why is being conscious of power. Giving people orders is quite different from inviting them to agree of their own will to do something. Everyone in an organization, no matter their role, can shift to an invitation mind-set whereby people determine if they will take part or not. Using clear purpose allows open invitation and personal leadership to flow.

Allowing people the choice of whether to do things or not might sound crazy to you. And if you start inviting people without making the purpose clear, it is. For example, if a colleague asked me if I could stay a few minutes extra to help clean the staff fridge, I might say no. I have things to do, and I don't use the fridge that much. But if my colleague told me that she knew someone who wanted to make a cake for everyone but was waiting until the fridge was cleaned, then I would receive the invitation differently. If she told me that the person who usually cleans the fridge had been on sick leave for a month was coming back the next day and it was a mess and everyone was out at a meeting, I would see the bigger picture and have the information in hand to make an informed decision. Horizontal culture creates the conditions for personal leadership to thrive by working with invitation with explicit purpose. It is a practice to offer the why and an invitation rather than expect people to simply execute.

Say I'm supporting a client who wants to start an organizational restructuring process. The client comes to us because they want it to be a collective process, not a management one. I walk them through it, how it needs also to be based on invitation. Here's the type of invitation people get:

> Here at XYZ Corporation, we are going to spend some time and energy to improve our structure. It's been 10 years since we last asked ourselves the question "What is the structure we want, we need, we dream of?" In that time we have tripled in size, our work has evolved, and the notion of management has changed as well. We need a structure that can carry us into the future and that feels aligned with who we are. We don't think that management should develop this on its own, and therefore we are planning a co-creation process in which *everyone* is invited. That means that you can decide if you want to actively participate in crafting this change or will happily accept the work of your colleagues. Do you want to participate? If so, the launch meeting is [date and time]. If you want to be involved, please come. If you are unable to make it and want to take part, please let us know.

The beautiful thing about an invitation is that people can actually say no. Inviting people allows everyone to see their attachments and expectations. It is a reminder that things that are a priority for you might not be a priority for other people. What's important is to work with those who show up.

Identify something, no matter how big or small, that you would like someone else to do. Formulate it as an invitation with a clear purpose. How will you feel if the person declines the invitation?

Keeping Purpose on Track

An organization's purpose can get neglected or lost. In vertical culture the assumption is that it is the role of management to keep purpose on track. Even when people clearly see that the organization is confused about purpose, they don't necessarily step up and act to clarify it. By contrast, in a horizontal culture people collectively strive to keep purpose on track. Anyone can support bringing a focus on purpose back. In fact, everyone has a responsibility to do that. Here are three ways you can help keep an organization on track with its purpose:

1. **Pick up on the signals.** Part of this practice involves picking up the signals that the organization is unclear about its purpose. Problems such as frustration, overdue deadlines, superfluous communication, and anxious attitudes can all be signals that there is an issue with the clarity of purpose.  Look out for these signals as a way of identifying that you need to activate your personal leadership. This is contributive and kind. If you are

demonstrating signals of confusion of purpose in your own work, let others know. It helps a group to develop a practice to pick up on the signals.

2. **Separate your personal preferences from the larger purpose.** Sometimes you will face a choice between the organization's purpose and your personal ideas or preferences. In those cases the organization's purpose always rules. So if you find yourself in a situation where you would prefer to be functioning in a different way than what is being suggested, there is no real reason to intervene and change things if the larger purpose is still on track.

3. **Engage your personal leadership.** When you notice confusion of purpose, it is time to support the path back to clarity of purpose. You can find a timely moment to make it known that you see the initiative might be off track and to remind yourself and others what the purpose is. To be able to do this does require that you stay tuned to the actual purpose without getting sidetracked with your personal preferences.

I REALIGN

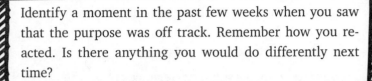

Identify a moment in the past few weeks when you saw that the purpose was off track. Remember how you reacted. Is there anything you would do differently next time?

Aligning with Purpose

When people understand and align with the why, they show up engaged. If you are aligned with the purpose of an initiative, you get energized to contribute to the work. When people are not connected to purpose, it can show in different ways. One red flag is that people make statements that begin with "I have to..." This indicates that the person feels like they are submitting to the command of another and that they have no choice to do otherwise.

Developing your own self-awareness about your alignment with purpose is a practice in itself. If you are unaware of how you stand, you can get caught up in a reactive or defensive mind-set that is not helpful for your state of mind or for the organization. Here is one way to check: Do you find yourself saying "I am working on this project" or "I have to work on this project"? If you think the project has value, you might-

feel you get to work on it. If you don't think it has value, you might begrudge your involvement in it. Remember to self-assess whether you are in alignment with the purpose of the initiatives you are engaged in.

Once you have gained self-awareness about your alignment with an initiative, you will be able to find a conscious way forward. You have three options:

1. **Accept the purpose.** If you are not aligned with the purpose, you can still choose to accept the purpose, to make peace with it. A friend of mine who works in finance put up a sign by his computer—"I choose to work here"—as a daily reminder that he had the freedom to leave, that he was not a prisoner. He chose this domain and place of work. He would face consequences if he left, but he had choices. What does purpose have to do with this? The more that people align with purpose, the more they will feel a powerful sense of personal agency.

2. **Intervene to modify the purpose.**
   If you are not in alignment with
   the purpose, you can intervene to
   bridge the gap by calling upon your
   personal leadership. In a recent
   training, I met a successful, engaged
   professional with some big questions.
   She was a newly appointed director
   in a large international nonprofit
   organization with a beautiful purpose
   that functioned hierarchically. She
   thought that the way her organization
   was working didn't feel right. She
   felt the disconnect between the
   purpose and the culture. She made
   a conscious decision to contribute to
   improving the alignment between
   the organizational culture and its
   purpose. In the same way, you can do
   this, although maybe at a lower level.
   If you feel a misalignment in the
   purpose of a policy, for example, you
   can make a proposal to adjust it.

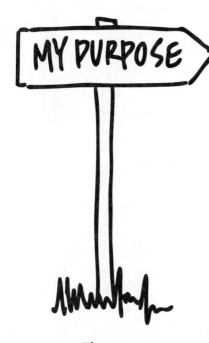

3. Move on. "What is the one thing I should be doing right now that feels right?" asked Frederic Laloux, the author of *Reinventing Organizations*, at an event in Montreal.[18] This question presents a different way of looking at purpose for yourself. By stepping away from the pressure of finding an answer to the huge question of "What is my purpose?" and bringing it to the here and now, you make it both more tangible and also more attainable—and therefore all the more scary. The more your organization's purpose comes alive, the more powerful the invitation will be for you to align with that culture. But if you see that you are not aligned with it, you can move on. I have a friend who is a participatory architect. She had a great job at a social housing firm but was miserable because of the firm's misalignment with purpose. Though the firm functioned with participatory ways with its clients, it did not do so with its employees. She left and eventually started her own firm with the following purpose: "Creating a built environment through collaboration." As she exemplifies, for some people the path forward is one of moving on.

Identify the purpose of a role you are responsible for, a project you are involved in, and your organization. How aligned are you with these three purposes? What is your approach to each (do you accept, intervene, move on)?

Purpose of the Organization

A final note on organizational purpose: The purpose of a non-hierarchical organization is *not* for its people to be happy. That is a by-product. The organization still has a deeper purpose that its business seeks to achieve. Usually, purpose is expressed in the form of its vision and mission statements. I am using the term *purpose* mostly because *vision* and *mission* have been used for purpose that is focused within the organization, rather than for a wider or deeper purpose that goes beyond the organization. The notion of purpose-driven organization is growing in popularity. In fact, many organizational mission statements are not really energizing or guiding organizations as they were meant to.[19] Organizations have gotten lost in self-preservation and the bottom line. By contrast, purpose-driven business—also known as conscious business—can ignite people's desire to contribute.

Discovering what the purpose of an organization should be can be challenging. I worked with a technology company, ET Group in Toronto. Their mission was to set up work spaces for good virtual communication. They realized that this purpose was not enlivening enough to carry the organization into the future and spent some time revisiting it. Their new purpose: "Unleashing the explosive potential of collaboration—transforming the way the most dynamic companies collaborate."

They now have a purpose that can drive the company into its next stage.

An organization that is clearly focused on purpose can recognize that competing organizations might be seen as part of the same movement and that they are working toward a common goal. If that is the case, it can make more sense for the organizations to pursue connection and collaboration.

 What is the purpose of your organization? Does the purpose feel energizing? Does it offer guidance?

Summary

There are practices that you can individually engage in to take responsibility to strengthen your own purpose-driven mind-set and that of your organization:

1. **Clarify purpose.** To clarify purpose you can simply stop and listen, get inspired, or go to the source where creation happened. Look to the birthing moment of an initiative to see its essential purpose.

2. **Invite rather than obliging.** Purpose is the essential information that allows people to consciously decide for themselves if they want to participate in an initiative. Letting them decide helps to liberate the organization from the obligation that is part of vertical culture.

3. **Keep purpose on track.** Tune in to the signals that inform you that purpose is off track, differentiate between your personal preferences and purpose, and engage your personal leadership.

4. **Align with purpose.** You can check in with yourself to see if you are aligned with the purpose of an initiative. Doing so develops your self-awareness and helps you make more conscious choices around your options: accept, intervene, or move on.

5. **Connect with the organization's purpose.** The purpose of the organization is neither to make its employees happy nor simply to be profitable. Within its domain an organization can and should be purpose driven. People want to work for and contribute to purpose-driven organizations.

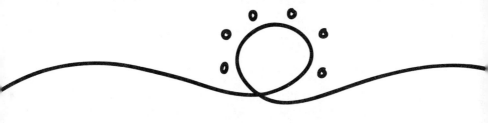

FIVE

MEETINGS

Sharing the Responsibilities and Accountability

We can be fully human and get lots of work done.
Ana from OuiShare Barcelona

Why Co-managing Meetings Is Important

Meetings are the backbone of organizational culture. They are pivotal to overall vision and growth, and no horizontal organization can thrive without a strong set of practices that guide meeting culture. Meetings are not only a place to get work done but also a place to build trust and relationships in an organization. When the relevance and attainment of meetings becomes a shared responsibility, they become, rather than a burden on everyone's time, a way to drive the organization forward.

In this chapter we explore practices to expand the responsibility and accountability of team meetings, including meeting starters, collective summarizing, and the use of silence and space. Meeting cultures differ from one organization to the next, so you will need to determine the practices that make sense for you and your organization.

A note on legal constraints: First, legal requirements typically apply to formal governance meetings such as general assemblies and board meetings. Other meetings such as committee meetings, team meetings, and work sessions are not legally bound. Second, in meetings where legal requirements apply, most of the legal requirements have little or no bearing on how a meeting is run. Voting rights do not dictate how decisions are made. The obligation to keep minutes does not specify how it should be done. Therefore, the formal meeting culture that many organizations follow may not be necessary. You might want to look at some other meeting practices that are supportive of a horizontal mind-set.

Co-managing Meetings Is Natural for Us

In our personal lives, we manage our meetings together quite well. We figure out our scheduling with one another. We'll meet on the computer, at the café, or in the park. When we get an invitation, we decide if we should attend. We even have meeting processes that feel generative of results. When you invite friends to a meeting, you might say something like, "Hey, let's figure out the details for our trip this weekend." This is an organic way of naming the intention for the meeting. Before we dive into the goal of the meeting, we often take time to connect with one another on a human level. We share updates on our children, our vacation, or our relationship, whatever fits the context. We care about everyone being heard. We organically determine if there are actions that

MEETING

need to be taken or deadlines that need to be made explicit. We even deal with issues of money. Together we manage the "meeting." In our personal lives, leadership flows among individuals. No one "chairs" the meeting. Indeed, if someone tries to chair a meeting in the personal realm, that person can be called "bossy."

The moment we begin using the term *meeting*, we suddenly stiffen up and feel we need to function in a way that we call *professional*, and the proceedings lose their collaborative feeling. In this chapter we look at different meeting practices for the work world, practices that help us get things done in a way that feels natural and enlivening. These are collaborative meeting practices: clarifying purpose together, checking in before jumping in, sharing equally, splitting up into subgroups, using silence to work better, setting the agenda, self-determining attendance, sharing the documentation, using the space to support co-managed meetings, and rotating the role of facilitator.

Clarifying Purpose Together

Taking a moment at the beginning of a meeting to collectively clarify why you are meeting and what you would like to accomplish sounds like a normal, natural thing to do, yet it is frequently passed over. In work meetings we are sometimes so eager to jump in to the topic that we don't revisit the why of the meeting. We assume that people know. However, reminding the group why the meeting is being held and what the group might expect to accomplish takes just a few seconds. Taking this moment is a precondition for a group to be collectively accountable for the success of a meeting. Without it, every other horizontal practice is weakened. Once the purpose is shared, anyone can raise questions and clear up any confusion. Everyone has the same information and can share responsibility for keeping the meeting on track. If you want to open team meetings to collective management, this is a foundational practice.

Think of a meeting you attended recently. Was the purpose stated clearly at the beginning? Was the expectation of what would be achieved explicit?

Checking In before Jumping In

The practice of beginning a meeting with a moment to check in with each other can't be emphasized enough. A check-in can look as simple as this: "How do we feel about this project right now?" Checking in helps dissipate outside distractions, engenders quality listening, and creates a general atmosphere that is authentic and therefore productive. Furthermore, checking in can open space for a new angle of exploration, loosen entrenched beliefs, or bring issues to the surface that might otherwise create discomfort and go unspoken.

Here are three important parts to the practice of checking in:

1. **Each person speaks from their own experience.** The check-in is not the time to intellectualize or analyze, just for each person to speak about what is coming up for them. It is a time for each person to connect with themselves. Each person speaks from where they are, as honestly as possible.

2. **No dialogue takes place.** Everyone simply witnesses what the others are saying. The topic of the meeting remains the focus of the meeting. No dialogue might take some practice, as people instinctively want to respond, commiserate, challenge, and offer support. The point is simply to listen, to silently acknowledge what has been said. The check-in is not the meeting.

3. **The amount of time needed can vary.** Sometimes a check-in should be carried out quickly, and other times a slow check-in is needed. The work can unfold like a lightning bolt thereafter. In creative work sessions, the check-in can take half the meeting because it becomes the creative springboard. It is a practice in and of itself to gauge the appropriate amount of time to accord to checking in.

Check-ins help us feel alive and present, so it is important to be thoughtful about the invitation and to avoid turning it into a routine. It is an art to finding the right question for that particular moment, configuration of people, purpose, or atmosphere. Here are some sample check-in questions:

- An event, such as a colleague's departure, has just taken place: "What are we letting go of?"

- The group is feeling stressed: "What do I need to leave at the door to be present today?" or "What do you need to know about me right now?"

- The team is facing a hurdle: "What is a recent frustration you have had, and how are you overcoming it?"

- The group wants to get creative about a topic, for example, trainings: "Name a training that inspired you recently and why."

At a two-hour meeting at my company, Percolab, we checked in around the question "What energy are you arriving with today?" The check-in took a full 20 minutes, but thereafter we were able deal efficiently with the meeting content: issues of acquisition, contractual agreements, communication, branding, and positioning.

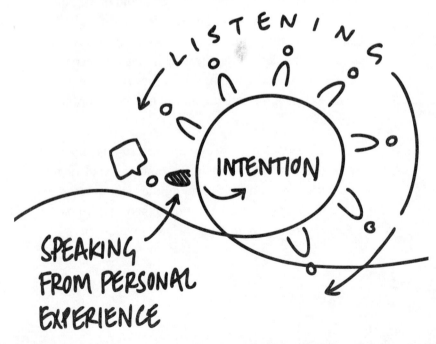

Remember, even though it is difficult, resist the tendency to react to anyone's comments during the check-in.

> Speak to the facilitator of a meeting you participate in. Get an agreement that for the next three meetings you can experiment with offering check-ins at the beginning of the meeting.

Sharing Equally

Going horizontal means that each person's voice in a meeting is equally valued. This is easier said than done because of our entrenched habits and tendencies. Here are four practices that can help you navigate the subtleties of sharing more equally:

1. **Be equally genuine and open.** If everyone else is revealing their real thoughts, you might want to do so as well. It is not time to start reformulating or commenting about what people have said until you have also revealed your own thoughts.

2. **Let others speak for themselves.**
When you speak, speak from your
own voice and perspective and leave
other people to speak from theirs.
Rather than saying "I agree with
what everyone has said..." or "There
is some validity in the different
opinions spoken so far," you might
say, "For me..." or "I think..."

3. **If you are the facilitator,
summarize regularly and rotate
the person who summarizes.** By
summarizing everyone's perspectives
and ideas, you lend authority to
yourself and others in a meeting.
Remember to let all voices be heard,
including your own, before you
summarize.

4. **Record the meeting visually.**
Record visually—on a flip chart,
whiteboard, or big paper on the
table—what everyone is saying as
the meeting progresses and make
the display in full view to all. Visual
recording equalizes and fosters
insights: when everyone sits together
with all that has been spoken, it
allows a new insight or idea to take
shape that wasn't there before.

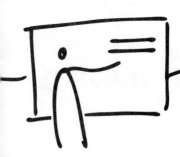

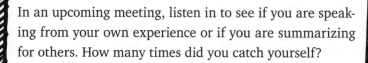

In an upcoming meeting, listen in to see if you are speaking from your own experience or if you are summarizing for others. How many times did you catch yourself?

Splitting Up into Subgroups

For some reason breaking into subgroups in a meeting can be difficult. We know what it's like when the group is no longer functional: the conversation becomes clunky, people begin to disengage, the same people speak all the time. Everyone feels the ineffectiveness, and yet no one gives themselves permission to propose that they break out into small groups. Instead, just say, "Hey, let's break into small groups for 15 minutes to explore some of these points and then come back together and share." It's so simple and so evident, yet it's rarely done. With a horizontal mind-set, you take responsibility for the success of the meeting, and therefore you can propose that the meeting break into small groups.

In a training I participated in at the European Cooperation in Science and Technology Association, employees worked in

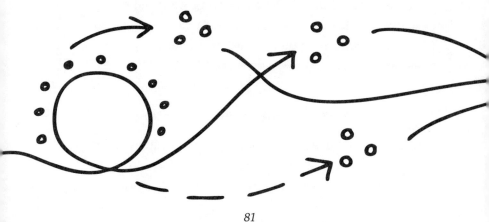

groups of 10 people on topics they had chosen. One of these groups took the initiative to divide into subgroups. It sounds so obvious, but at the time it can be hard to do. Needless to say, when we regrouped to share the results of the work, the group that had split up had accomplished by far the most work, even going so far as to draft actionable points. Furthermore, this group seemed the most enlivened and energized. It can be exhausting to spend time in a group that is too big to do the work that needs to get done.

So how do we know when it makes sense to break out into groups and when it is important to stay together? My answer is to listen inside yourself. Just considering that smaller groups may be an effective alternative will free you to look for moments where this strategy could be effective. When you start to feel frustrated by the meeting and its ineffectiveness, that might mean something is misaligned. Then it's time.

> The next time you feel frustrated about the ineffectiveness of a group too large for the work at hand, take the initiative and invite the group to break out into small groups. Make sure to offer a clear time limit and purpose so that people may self-organize, and reassure people that the group will share their results at the end.

Using Silence to Work Better

In our personal lives, we seek out peace and quiet and treasure it. Yet in our work world where we need productivity and performance, we think silence serves no purpose. But silence can help us go beneath the surface and go to the deeper source of issues and the more truthful places within ourselves. Silence is useful. The term *think time* was coined by researcher Robert J. Stahl, who documented the importance of silence to allow the human brain time to process information and feelings.[20] If a meeting stalls on a challenging question, silence might mean that people are deeply engaging with the question. Since we are not used to silence, some people might interpret the silence as "something is wrong," or as "no one is stepping up," so they begin talking, when the silence was actually helping the group. We can help one another feel more comfortable with silence.

MOMENT OF SILENCE

You can easily slip silence into any work session. For example, when you invite your colleagues to share their thoughts on a topic, you might say, "Let's take 20 seconds in silence to consider this question before we begin sharing." When you do this, the quality of the conversation, both the listening and speaking, will go up. Or the next time you experience an awkward silence in a meeting, you might gently suggest that the silence is good and might be helping the work. Just naming it can release the awkwardness. Or if someone has experienced emotion, you might want to invite a moment of silence so everyone can collect themselves. If you want to go further, invite everyone to close their eyes and take a moment to reflect on what they are leaving with from the meeting or day (don't force anyone, though). Closed eyes help us be in silence. Surprisingly enough, people actually appreciate a moment of silence at work.

> Step up in a meeting to propose that the group take a moment of silence. You might ask for a moment for everyone to think quietly before opening up the conversation. Explain that it helps everyone stay focused on the collective purpose.

Setting the Agenda

In horizontal culture no one individual can have a view on all that needs to be addressed, so setting a meeting agenda is usually a collective process. Furthermore, we can work more deliberately with the way agendas are set. Meeting agenda items can be divided into three categories: (1) agenda items that *recur*, (2) agenda items that are set *prior* to the meeting, and (3) agenda items that are set *during* the meeting. In a horizontal culture, we try to deliberate and be intentional about how agendas are set.

Recurring agenda items, those that automatically come back each meeting, can be useful for creating rituals and saving time. For example, if you want to keep a meeting short and to the point, a stand-up meeting with a fixed agenda is ideal. Everyone stays standing while each person takes a minute to share (1) what they worked on yesterday, (2) the status of that work, (3) what they are working on today, and (4) where they are stuck or require help.

Recurring agenda items can also be used to grow a new cultural practice. If you want to develop your culture of feedback, you could have a recurring agenda item of giving one another feedback using some of the practices in chapter 8. Doing that for a few months can change a culture.

The facilitator of a traditional meeting often reserves a short time at the end for "all other business." Unsurprisingly, the "all other business" segment of a meeting is the agenda item that most frequently balloons out of its limits. In certain contexts you might want to set some or even all of the agenda *during* the meeting, rather than just having 10 minutes of open session. Setting the agenda during the meeting allows for both flexibility and structure. Here's a way to help you know when that form of agenda setting is appropriate: If a meeting is about implementation and logistics or topics that have lots of things that are known up front, then it might be appropriate to set the agenda *prior* to the meeting. But if a meeting requires creativity, innovation, and learning, or anytime there is lack of clarity prior to the meeting, then it might be appropriate to set the agenda at the beginning of the meeting.

Establishing an agenda in the meeting, if used in the right context, can have a huge positive impact on effectiveness. When given space and an invitation to do so, people know how to bring organizational priorities to a meeting. Not knowing beforehand the topics that will be addressed can feel uncomfortable, but at the same time it can feel very enlivening. It definitely develops our capacity to trust.

So how do we set agendas during a meeting? One way is what I call the "agile agenda approach":

I. Clarify the theme of the meeting: for example, project management learnings, business development experimentation, or operations optimization. This theme can be shared prior to the meeting.

2. At the beginning of the meeting, invite those who have a topic they would like to discuss to write their name, topic, time required, and number of people required on the whiteboard or flip chart. Each person who puts their name up is responsible for facilitating their topic.

Theme: Learning from Our Work

Name	Subject	Minutes	People
Jolene	Branding for client: Acme Corp. after-action review	10	2
Adam	New meetings process	5	all
Serena	Publicity about the co-working space	5	4
Jenny	My presentation in Switzerland	10	2
. . .			

3. Begin the meeting with a short topic with a quick win. A quick win will get everyone into the flow of the meeting, and you can move on from there. Remember, whoever put their name up is responsible for facilitating their point.

When you use this approach, people are fearful that topics will be missed or that there won't be enough time. However, over the years I have seen that it usually works itself out quite well—just like when we self-organize our "meetings" with friends and family members, the meeting participants self-organize and discuss. For example, if someone states that there is not enough time for their topic and they consider it urgent, someone else may volunteer to shorten their time to make time available for their co-worker. The agile agenda approach is a practice to identify topics that are important for the organization and to facilitate a productive and timely process with your colleagues.

Another form of agile agenda is to work with one or two fixed time slots in meetings. Individuals name a topic they want to facilitate and point to where they will be in the room. The facilitators go to their designated spaces, and everyone is free to move around as they wish. In what is known as "the law of two feet," each individual takes responsibility to be somewhere where they can learn or contribute.

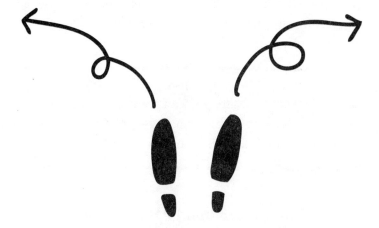

At the end of the allotted time, the group reunites to share feedback about what happened in each subgroup.

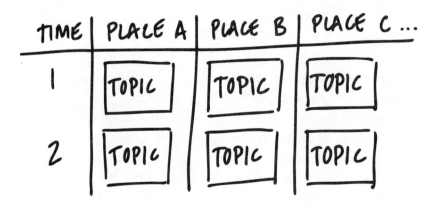

This approach is part of a larger movement known as "Open Space Technology."[21] It is used throughout the world with groups from 5 to 2,000 and for short meetings to multiday events!

In a horizontal culture, if someone is feeling agitated with the way agendas are created, they can propose a change or experiment with a different approach. Part of the challenge in suggesting changes is having a wider understanding of all that is possible.

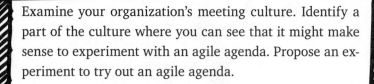

Examine your organization's meeting culture. Identify a part of the culture where you can see that it might make sense to experiment with an agile agenda. Propose an experiment to try out an agile agenda.

Self-Determining Attendance

The holy grail of horizontal culture might be the ability of employees to self-determine attendance at meetings. Employees like being able to have autonomy to decide if they need to attend a meeting. The practice of self-determined meeting attendance leads to greater efficiency for organizations, greater satisfaction by employees, and greater ease and skill for employees when deciding where to be at any given time.

An organization requires a basic but well thought out framework for self-determined attendance to work. Here are two examples of structures I have seen:

1. A team holds short stand-up meetings twice a week to quickly share information; all sit-down meetings are optional. Organizers of sit-down meetings make explicit three things for each meeting: (1) the purpose of the meeting, (2) the expected output of the meeting, and (3) the required presence of any person or particular expertise. With this information individuals can self-select if they need to or will attend.

2. Everyone must attend, physically or virtually, 70 percent of team meetings. If any individual can't attend, they must (1) inform their colleagues, and (2) read the notes online.

The appropriate structure needs to be created with the specific context as a guide, and it should be co-created. Finding the appropriate structure can take a few tries to get it right.

At a European agency in Belgium, the director attended all interdepartmental meetings. At one point he noted that it would make more sense if those people closest to the work attended the meetings. This generated lots of reaction at first because executives customarily met together to discuss things among themselves and then would pass the information on to the appropriate people in their respective teams. Because the director trusted the employees to have access to strategy discussions concerning them, he was released from this obligation. The division subsequently increased its effectiveness.

With just a few simple mechanisms in how meetings are run, a horizontal culture can allow more autonomy, agency, and shared power.

Run a small experiment with self-determined attendance and afterward have a conversation with those who came to the meeting and those who didn't. What reactions did people have to being able to determine for themselves if they would show up at a meeting? What could be the ideal framework for meeting attendance at your organization?

Sharing the Documentation

If we want a meeting to be co-managed, we must make documenting it a shared responsibility. Here are three aspects to this practice.

I. **Documentation responsibility.** Documenting meetings can be a shared responsibility. As a meeting starts, anyone can offer to contribute to the documentation. If a team wants to foster a new culture, it can require that everyone have a turn documenting. If the team has a hierarchy of any kind still at play, make sure that the responsibility does not fall to the lowest-ranking employee present to always take the notes.

2. **Documentation tools.**
   Technology offers us
   many novel ways to share
   documentation. Online
   cloud-based documenting
   tools (such as Google Docs,
   Dropbox, and Evernote)
   make sharing documentation easy. As an added bonus,
   participants who attend virtually can follow along in
   real time. Just taking the documentation into an online
   space, rather than keeping it on one person's computer,
   is a more horizontal approach. It makes access and
   readability easier because notes can be accessed directly
   online rather than through a PDF that needs to be
   opened.

3. **Documentation**
   structure. Meetings
   comprise different
   elements: open
   discussion, clarification,
   dissemination of key
   information, assignment
   of action points and responsibilities, and of course
   decision making. In horizontal culture you want to
   make it as easy as possible for people to get a quick
   view of what happened at the meeting. You might
   want to separate the notes into two sections: key
   points that you want everyone to see at a glance, and
   all the rest. Each organization or team needs to find a

method of documentation that suits their context. At Percolab we have a decision log in which we record decisions as a way to help everyone keep abreast of new organizational decisions. It's fabulous.

> Set up a method of shared documentation and experiment with sharing the notes of a meeting with at least one other person.

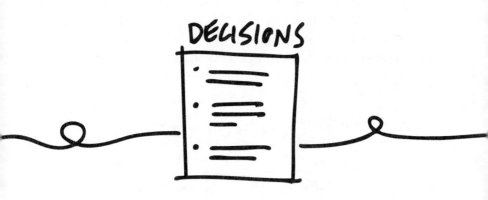

Using the Space to Support Co-managed Meetings

Where people sit in a meeting directly affects the power dynamics. If there is an official head of the table or if the person who chairs the meeting sits at the same place every time, this seat is loaded with power. To share responsibility for the success of the meeting, you can physically embody that idea. Simply invite people to sit where they haven't sat before, or rotate the seating. Changing the seating is easy enough, though doing so may elicit some eye rolling before people experience how impactful it can be.

If your team's power dynamics are stuck, change the meeting room, or try holding your meeting without a table. I recommend no table as the simplest way to change established dynamics.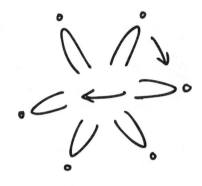

We associate sitting in a circle with group therapy, so don't be surprised if you get a few comments about that. In the circle people are both vulnerable and open, and this can be good for meetings.

Tiimiakatemia University in Jyvaskyla, Finland, has an amazing entrepreneurial program that has spread throughout the world. What struck me when I visited the university was that no matter where I went on the campus, the rooms were set up with chairs on wheels in circles—with any tables in the room along the walls. Everyone was working in a circle all the time. I witnessed with my own eyes the efficiency of the circle.

> Try holding a team meeting without tables or in a new location. The first time, people will typically struggle with focus because our brains associate a work environment with a conventional meeting room. This is why it is important to hold the meeting in that space three times. By the third time, the novelty will have worn off, and you will begin to sense the difference in quality that a change in the space offers.

Rotating the Role of Facilitator

All humans need to be able to take on the role of facilitator at times. This does not mean everyone needs to have professional facilitator skills, but we should acknowledge that being a facilitator is part of life and helps us be better leaders at work, at home, and with our friends. And rotating the role of facilitator in meetings is a key non-hierarchical practice.

People who disengage at meetings completely flip their attitudes once they themselves take on the role of facilitator. The person who usually leads is invited to step back from that role, and in so doing they create space for others to develop their leadership. The entire meeting takes on better energy with the engagement of a new facilitator.

Taking on the role of facilitator for the first time can be scary for people, so everyone needs to be supportive and kind to one another. Rotating the facilitator role might be considered important enough that an organization would formally embed the practice into its employee handbook. Some organizations might even consider it an important enough function to track.

> If you typically facilitate meetings, step down and create space for someone else. If you typically do not facilitate meetings, step up and ask to facilitate one. Just try out something new.

Summary

Meetings are an ideal place to grow a horizontal culture. A variety of practices can help make meetings more collaborative egalitarian, and efficient:

1. **Clarify purpose together.** At the beginning of a meeting, make sure the purpose is clear.

2. **Check in before jumping in.** Check-ins help a meeting be more fluid and efficient because everyone is present.

3. **Share equally.** Be as open as others, let everyone speak for themselves, rotate summarizing, and work visually.

4. **Split up into subgroups.** Anyone can sense the need to break into subgroups and make it happen.

5. **Use silence to work better.** Invite silence in to support the quality of the meeting.

6. **Set the agenda.** Know different ways to set an agenda and when to change the type of agenda you're using.

7. **Self-determine attendance.** Allowing people the choice to attend a meeting can enhance efficiency and employee satisfaction.

8. **Share the documentation.** Share the work of documenting meetings.

9. **Use the space.** Use chairs and space design to embody egalitarian meetings.

10. **Rotate the role of facilitator.** Allowing everyone to facilitate the meeting is a form of shared leadership and helps to get people engaged in a meeting.

SIX

TRANSPARENCY

Open Is Effective and Efficient

Transparency is the new objectivity.
David Weinberger

Openness and transparency foster trust, initiative taking, and fairness. They are foundational for a horizontal culture. Being open means there is nothing to hide. Suspicions fall away, and people are able to form trusting relationships. If we want people to actively take care of the organization and fully engage, we need to treat one another as capable adults who can have access to information about what is going on. In a horizontal culture, information is shared throughout the organization. When information is shared, people engage less in behaviors of manipulation and self-centeredness and more in actions that are ethical, caring, and equitable.

When I say "transparency," I am not referring to sharing synthetic information with your colleagues but actively and openly providing access to information about unfinished and imperfect work, throughout the organization and, when appropriate, even beyond the organization. Transparency is about inviting people in to the real data rather than keeping them away from it, even if doing so makes you uneasy. It is about overcoming your discomfort about potentially being criticized and questioned. Transparency affects many aspects of how we work and how we relate to one another. Though we value the concept of openness and transparency, we come from a strong tradition of closed practices and rules. For most of us, the practice of transparency lags behind the importance we give to it.

In this chapter we explore three types of practices: (1) growing your sharing culture, (2) inviting in the external world, and (3) getting beyond taboos around finances.

Transparency as a Normal Human Practice

As human beings we are naturally open with one another in our personal lives. We share our thoughts and ideas every day: "My vacation was great." "That train trip was awful." By sharing with one another, we make sense of events that transpire, whether it's a breakup or a life transition. By making ourselves heard, we invite compassion and solidarity. We know how to ask for specific information: "Where did you get those shoes?" "What did you think of that movie?" We even share our thoughts about money: "How expensive was that restaurant?" "Is your new mattress good value for the money?" We like helping one another get a good deal.

Sometimes we share more with friends and family and sometimes with people we just met. We share on the internet what we've learned about how to set up a mouse trap, peel a mango, or repair a leaky pipe. Millions of people have contributed to the 44 million pages of content in English-language Wikipedia, as well as the almost 300 other versions in other languages.[22] These numbers are testimony to how sharing is natural for humans.

We even like to share physical spaces. For centuries we have opened our homes to travelers. A modern version of this tradition is "couch surfing," in which people stay in one another's homes across the planet. Another way we share space is in the co-working movement, where people share office space.

We also tend to know that some things are better not shared or need to be carefully shared. We know when to steer clear of delicate topics and situations or when to use our knowledge wisely. We know that people have different levels of comfort around openness and transparency, and we naturally adjust ourselves. We are naturally skilled in being open and transparent with one another.

Growing Your Sharing Culture

"Would you mind sharing that report?" "Can you show me that budget?" These questions are daily fare in the workplace, where we know the value of sharing. I spent three years working on an ambitious information-sharing project with the European Commission. The premise was simple enough. In the realm of taxation and customs, the national administration of each member state was faced with similar challenges. If officials of each nation could openly share, optimization could happen at a system-wide level. The benefits for all of Europe would be huge, from quality of activities to financial savings. In addition to the task of developing the online systems to support information sharing, we also had to facilitate the cultural shift for taxation and customs officials. When you are changing practices relating to transparency, the cultural shift is just as important as the processes. Bringing greater transparency to a work context can be fraught with nerves, emotion, and fear. It is important to work through this aspect of the shift as well as the logistics. Today, 10 years later, the site is still in use and inviting in new members.[23] Let's examine ways to create a sharing culture.

Default to Open

Most of us aren't aware that in organizations we default to a "closed" position. That is, we keep things closed or private "just in case." It is possible to change your default functioning around sharing. Shifting to a "default to open" approach, does *not* mean everything is open; it just means that if there is no good reason to keep it closed, then it is de facto shared.

It also means you don't need to justify why it is open. The personal practice here is to be self-aware about your reflex to keep something private, and then to distinguish between personal discomfort and organizational benefit.

Despite the importance of privacy, organizations are calling for more agility and more flow of information. More than that, society is calling for more agility and flow of information between organizations. The US consultancy firm August is an example of the emerging sharing culture in business.[24] Its internal files are open to the general public, and they include operating agreements, salaries, capitalization tables, governance and policies, teams, roles, accountabilities, intellectual property about how they do their work, and organizational tools. By sharing openly August is contributing to creating a sharing culture where organizations share externally. You never know who will pick up what, and that's okay. Clearly, being transparent is working for August, as the company continues to grow.

When your methods, learning, resources, and meetings are shared, they can actually contribute in unknown ways across your organization and beyond. In some organizations meetings are video recorded so that people may, for whatever reason, refer back to them. Such recording isn't new. The videos of the team retreat of the computer and software company NeXT in 1985 and 1986 with Steve Jobs has been viewed more than 2 million times.[25]

Sharing organizational information may be a good thing, but what about people bringing their challenges, errors, and problems to everyone's attention? Being open and honest about your challenges, errors, and problems, no matter the scale or type, is part of an adult, accountable culture. In

horizontal culture you take responsibility for your mistakes and use them as fodder for learning. And sharing with your colleagues and other teams or departments may also be a good thing, but what about sharing with your wider community of clients and partners, and what about sharing with the general public? If we want to optimize at a system level, then we will need to start sharing even our errors outside our organizations. But let's start by acknowledging that it is not easy and will require practice.

> Think of a specific work method, work meeting, or work policy that is close to you. If you were to take a default-to-open approach, would you make any change in how these items are shared? How would you feel if you made the change?

Make It Easy for Others

While ease of use is rarely considered, it is one of the most overlooked elements in creating greater transparency in an organization. Think about the experience of those who will be accessing information. You want access to be easy. For example, PDF files are difficult to modify or use as a springboard for innovation. If you want to give people the ability to use information, then think through the flow of their access and their ability to use the information. Is the way you are sharing the information helpful for other people to be able to use the information within their context? Here are three questions to ask:

1. Do people need permission to access the information?
2. Can people grant access to other people?
3. Do the file format or permissions give editing rights?

Identify a specific item in your work that you feel you are open and transparent with. It might be a report, a method, or meeting notes. Identify in detail how widely you are sharing the item and how supportive you are being in sharing it (permission to access, to grant permission to others, to edit).

Make Your Daily Activities Visible to Your Colleagues

Knowing what your colleagues are up to is important in any kind of organization, and even more so in a non-hierarchical one. Team communication spaces (also known as team chat, these are digital workspaces for people to engage in conversation and find content) are revolutionizing the workplace with a light and fluid way of communicating with all people in the system. The chat channels or rooms afford quick and easy communication, allowing members to know what others are doing without any extra effort. All that is required is that colleagues, instead of speaking privately, move their conversation to a group communication space.

Team communication spaces are an organic way of letting people know what is going on and creating room for collective interaction. At Percolab I might post the following message in our channel for ongoing projects: "@paul Are you available to go over the visual approach for our strategy meeting with client X this Friday?" When I post in this way, others are informed of the project and the way it is taking shape without making any extra effort. My question "@meghan Can you choose a photo for the new portfolio item for my bid to client Y?" goes in the business development channel. We even have a channel called "Percolab in action," where we share photos, videos, and thoughts about what's going on. "Just taking train back from the Beyond Hierarchy event in Toronto. Thinking how we could do a similar event in Montreal."

#PERCOLAB-IN-ACTION

 Sam 2.03pm

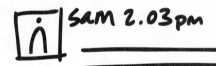

There are other methods that help us share with our colleagues about the work we are doing in a timely fashion. The stand-up meeting, created by the agile software development movement, has spread into other organizational areas because the methodology is so smart. As described in chapter 5, it is a quick catch-up without any chairs. No risk of the meeting dragging on if you can't sit down! The stand-up meeting has a protocol for the process that the group agrees on. For example, each person has one minute to share (not discuss) (1) what they worked on yesterday, (2) the status of that work, (3) what they are working on today, and (4) where they need help. The frequency for stand-up meetings can vary, from three to four times a day during periods of intensive production to once a week in less active periods. The frequency always depends on the context as the organization seeks to blend the meetings with the natural rhythm of the work. The sharing that happens in these meetings means that bottlenecks are revealed, people can help one another get unstuck, and peers help one another stay on track and motivated.

> At the end of every day, how much do the people in your team know what you were working on? What are the practices that you use to bring others into your daily work world?

Proactively Invite in the External World

In hierarchical culture the default modality is to keep your work to yourself, not to let others in. This reserve may be to protect intellectual property or to preserve a sense of security. We struggle to imagine that there could be value to opening our work to people from other departments, organizations, or even fields. But transparency can and should extend to people who are outside your own organization. Here are some of the values and benefits of this level of transparency and openness:

1. **Collective intelligence.**
   People from diverse
   disciplines might offer
   insights, connections,
   ideas, questions,
   experience, and creativity
   that would be helpful to
   your work and challenges.

   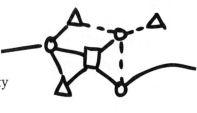

2. **Community.** By opening
   up with people who might
   want to discover your
   organization, you connect
   with them in an organic
   way. Because opening up
   requires trust, it builds
   relationships that are
   based on integrity.

3. **System thinking.**
   Being open helps an
   organization step away
   from an us versus them
   mind-set and step into an
   interdependent system
   mind-set. For a purpose-
   driven organization
   that wants to work
   systemically, it makes
   sense to invite the system
   in and to collaborate with
   others.

To do transparency well, a practice should be repeated regularly, because we are not used to it. No matter what form your transparency takes, you will need to observe these three guiding principles:

1. **Invite with reciprocity.** Let people know why they are being invited in. Ensure that the experience is a mutually beneficial one. With practice the benefits get easier to see and name.

2. **Stay on track.** When a group meets that is not part of an established team, it is more challenging to hold the purpose of the activity. The facilitator should specify the purpose and the time allowed. If someone starts telling a long anecdote, it is your job to maintain the boundary of the activity.

3. **Value external input.** You will want to make it known to guests that their thoughts and ideas have value and you want to hear them, and that outside perspectives often bring refreshing angles to the work.

You can practice transparency informally by talking about your work with someone who is external to the organization. Even passing moments can be opportunities, such as when you meet someone who is visiting your organization or whom you meet at an event. You might need to fight off your reflex to think that they won't be interested or have anything to contribute. If you can approach an exchange with a clear invitation, a specific purpose, and a willingness to let the person know you value their thoughts and ideas, how can it go wrong? All of us need to start getting better at working more openly with others. We need a mind-set shift.

You can also practice transparency more formally within a project. At Percolab we have external guests at our team meetings: clients, members of the wider communities we are part of, researchers who are connected to our work, professionals in transition who are trying out our organizational culture, or job candidates. Sometimes they help us brainstorm; other times they bring in useful information from the ecosystem. They always keep us in check.

In my work with the French government (at the Centre national de la fonction publique territoriale), I train public employees to leave their offices and go into the field, to observe government from a user's perspective, to listen and learn what is needed and desired rather than assuming or projecting. This fieldwork involves proactively connecting with the external world in a way that can completely transform a working culture.

> Think of two recent meetings you attended. Think through everything that was discussed at those meetings. Do you see any reason that someone from the outside could not have attended the meetings? Do you see that someone from the outside could have made a positive contribution?

Overcoming Taboos around Finances

Organizations with a vertical mind-set tend to treat finances as a loaded topic, off limits to all but a few. In a vertical culture, the organization keeps important money information in the hands of management and away from employees. In a horizontal culture, being open and transparent about money is foundational so that employees can be fully engaged with the organization.

The transparency practices involve overcoming the tendency to treat financial information like a taboo and approaching them as data. (Your own attitude toward money and trust will be called into play on the topic of transparency and finances.) The practices include transparency with financial information, both internally with your colleagues and externally with clients, partners, and even the public. Transparency comes into play in information about (1) budgets and bookkeeping, (2) profit margins and pricing, and of course (3) salaries.

Budgets and Bookkeeping

We can practice examining our assumptions around transparency in financial information. In vertical culture, access to the organization's financial information is restricted to those who have direct need for the information. In horizontal culture access to the organization's financial information is shared as widely as possible. If you have access to the information, you might get uncomfortable sharing it, and if you don't have access to financial information, you might feel included and trusted if the information is shared.

We need to be conscious of our reflexive boundaries around financial information and shift them as needed to step into a horizontal culture. You might be in a position to give access to financial information, or you might make a request to gain access to financial information.

When people have access to budget information around projects, they can learn how to work with and keep within budgets. When they have access to company budgeting information for expenses such as office supplies, furniture, and rental costs, they feel more accountable and involved. And another level of transparency is to give people access to the organization's accounting system. This level is possible with online accounting systems that can be configured to offer view-only access. These are a few of the many possibilities to offer access.

> If you have access to the organization's budgets and book-keeping, think of financial information that you could experiment with sharing. Do it.
>
> If you don't have access to budgets and bookkeeping, identify financial information you would like to know and why. Now request that information with someone in the organization who could make access available.

Profits and Pricing

In vertical culture the way an organization determines the pricing of its products and services is considered confidential information. In horizontal culture a different worldview sees power in sharing such information, internally and even externally.

Here are three ways in which information about profits and pricing can be shared:

1. **Sharing with employees.** If employees have access to full information on pricing, they can engage more fully  in the details that leverage profit margins and pricing strategies. Additionally, if employees are not given this information, they can hold on to inaccurate assumptions and distrust.

2. **Sharing with clients.** Some organizations have begun using transparent pricing models with their clients. They break through all the opacity around pricing and profit margins by specifying them up front.

3. **Sharing in procurement.** Some organizations have procurement processes that specify up front the available budget in their requests for proposals, calls for tender, and quotes. Rather than focusing on guessing the budget, the organization and supplier focus is on the process and approach that are possible within the budget.

A new phenomenon known as the "shared economy" is challenging conventional notions of how trainings and conferences are paid for. Instead of paying a fixed amount up front, participants pay a nominal fee up front and agree to an additional fee later based on the value they perceive from the activity, the financial data they receive about the activity, and the financial capacity they have to pay.

Here is how it works: Near the end of the event, participants are provided the budget details for the event including amounts for provisions (with projected honorariums for organizers) and a summary of monies received. Then a few calculations are made and shared: For an ideal budget where organizers obtain full rate, what would be the average payment per person? With the monies received, what is the average price per person? This allows people to know if they are causing a financial stress on the organization or not. Then, with this information people are invited to pay an additional amount if they wish. There are no right answers, actions, or feelings for this practice. People tend to love it, and at the same time, they feel terribly uncomfortable. We are not used to having access to so much information and agency around money.

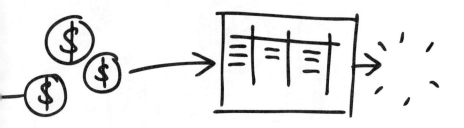

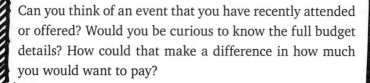

Can you think of an event that you have recently attended or offered? Would you be curious to know the full budget details? How could that make a difference in how much you would want to pay?

Transparent Salaries

The thorniest hot spot in financial transparency is compensation. Compensation gets at the very root of a hierarchical system, in which someone else gets to determine the value of your work. While the manager knows everyone's salary, colleagues do not know one another's salaries.

There is a growing movement to make salaries transparent. Companies like Buffer, a mobile app developer, share their salary calculator online.[26] Pay equity initiatives, brought about by men's greater ease at negotiating their salaries, are inviting increased transparency around salaries.

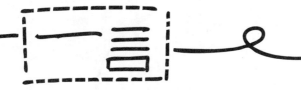

Fitzii, a Canadian recruitment firm, recently shifted to transparent and self-determined salaries.[27] The way they did this was to invite all employees to write a letter to themselves explaining how much they thought they should earn and then share the letter with a colleague for feedback. This prepared everyone for a company meeting dedicated to discussing the new policy. At the meeting they went around the circle and each person named how much they would like to earn. The numbers were added up, the total was compared with the actual available budget for salaries, and the difference made known. They went around the circle a second time and allowed everyone to adjust their salary based on the information they then knew. Interestingly, the total amount requested the second time around came in under budget. In this case, allowing employees to self-set salaries reduced the value of salary increases requested.

On a scale of 1 to 10 how much do you feel your salary is fair? How would you feel if your colleagues knew your salary? Do you think if you knew your colleagues' salaries, you would feel more or less financial stress and anxiety?

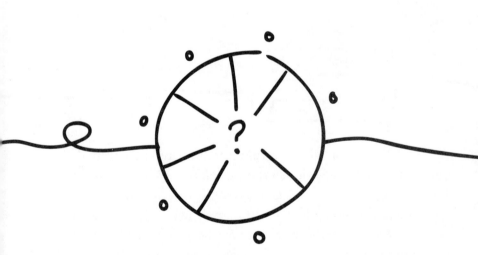

Summary

Organizations are calling for more agility and the free flow of information. This does not mean that we need to be transparent and open with everything, but we do need to shift from the reflex to shield information to a mind-set of openness. You need to find your way to developing your ease with increased transparency. In this chapter we looked at three aspects of openness and transparency:

1. **Grow your sharing culture.** Switch to open-by-default thinking and be more conscious about what you are sharing, how wide you are sharing, and how easy you can make your sharing for others. Share information about what you create and produce, what your activities are, and what your mistakes and challenges are.

2. **Invite in the external world.** When you invite in the outside world, you increase the collective intelligence, enhance a sense of community, and stimulate system thinking. These are deliberate ways of maintaining value and reciprocity.

3. **Get beyond taboos around finances.** Shift your boundaries around sharing information about budgets and bookkeeping, about pricing practices internally and externally, about shared-economy payment practices with clients, and about the thorny topic of transparent salaries.

No matter what your role is in the organization, you will find that the practice of transparency can be uncomfortable. Transparency is a practice you need to work at to strengthen.

SEVEN

DECISION MAKING

Sharing the Power

*Living is a constant process of deciding
what we are going to do.*
José Ortega y Gasset

Why Sharing Decision Making Is Important

"Should we hire that person?" "What's the best price point on that product?" Decision making and organizational life go hand in hand. Decision making is what keeps an organization moving forward. How can employees be fully engaged in an organization if they are not part of its decision making? In fact, if organizations are serious about cultivating an adult-to-adult partnership culture where accountability stands strong and tall over blame and victimization, participation in decision making is how it happens. When people are involved in decision-making processes, people who make the decision champion the decision. As the saying goes, "If it's about us, don't do it without us."

When people throughout an organization participate in making decisions, more collective intelligence is harnessed. The more people develop their ease and capacity to make decisions and be accountable for them, the more an organization can be nimble and wise. What would happen if anyone in the organization could make proposals? What would happen if everyone could be trusted within their zone of action and expertise to make good decisions for themselves and for the organization?

Unfortunately, decision making is also the number one source of friction and frustration in organizations. No wonder organizations are nervous about spreading it around. People misunderstand shared decision making, believing it to be a long and painful process of reaching consensus. In this chapter we delve into practices that will help develop your organization's capability to share decision making.

We Share Decision Making Every Day

We barely even notice all the different ways we navigate decision making. We know some decisions, like deciding to get married, are better made together. Other decisions, like when our grown children and their spouses choose to have children, are best left to others. Sometimes, we can be in an in-between decision space: "I don't care what stove we buy as long as it's electric."

We navigate group decisions by alternating between the collective and the individual. A group of hikers needs to choose between one trail and another. Some hikers make suggestions, others state their preferences, and others just go with the flow. The decision that most people agree on is taken.

We know how to invite another person's advice when we're making a decision. "What do you think?" I text my husband a photo of me in a dress I might buy. I'm asking for advice, but we both know that the final decision is mine.

We know when the time is ripe for a decision. We sit with the possibilities, research it, talk it out, and know when it's time to choose. We know if we have been impulsive or if we have been procrastinating.

We know decisions can be wrong. It's not the end of the world. We share decision making in natural ways and deal with friction around decisions regularly. We know how to figure out if we want to make a decision on our own, to make a decision with others, or to not get involved. We also know if it makes sense to invite in advice from others or not.

Our Beliefs and Fears around Decision Making

We know that when people are involved in decisions that affect them, they feel a greater sense of belonging to the organization.

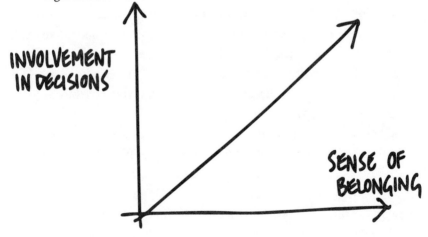

Despite what we know about getting people involved in decision making, in hierarchical culture, those with authority make decisions on behalf of others. But the model for decision making is changing. Our workplaces and our democratic institutions are becoming more participatory. More and more often, organizations are consulting employees before a new change initiative is officially announced and executed. Going horizontal has a lot to do with widening input into decision making—both internally within the organization and externally with stakeholders.

The New Economics Foundation has a typology of participation that helps to ascertain all that we can be doing together:

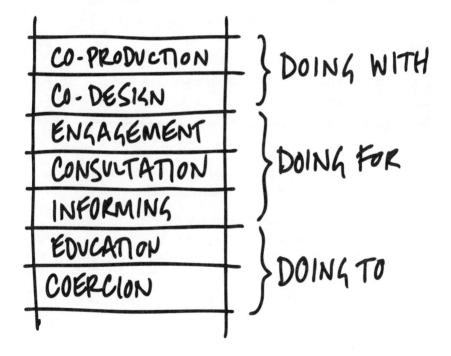

Organizations must learn ways of opening up decision-making processes that are efficient and productive. This is new for many organizations. Recently, I supported a process with a chartered professionals association to develop a new competency framework for the profession. The framework codifies what the profession wants its future to be, and training, certification, and inspection will need to align to it. It was the first time this process was being done in a co-creative way, with members and nonmembers of the association. The value was clear for the association: better results and better relationships. With a wider participation, the association gains collective intelligence, and the competency framework will be a true reflection of the concerns and aspirations of the field. With hundreds of people taking part in the process, the framework will have strong anchoring.

> Where do you personally stand on the idea of working in co-creation? Is your stance the same as that of your organization?

Using the Appropriate Method
for a Given Situation

Even though the decision-making process is rather informal in our personal lives, it requires some thinking through in the work world. Different decision-making methods have their place and purpose within an organization. The table below shows different methods and notes on the context for their use.[28]

Differentiating Decision Making Methods

	Control	Accountability	Participation	Speed
Autocratic	individual	decision maker	none	fastest
Majority vote	collective	collective	yes (but superficial)	fast
Advice process	individual	decision maker	yes	fast
Consent	collective	collective	yes	fast
Consensus	collective	collective	yes	slow

Examples of when it is useful

Autocratic: in chaotic situations where there is no time to consult

Majority vote: in simple situations that require speedy decisions and quick consultation

Advice process: when the situation is complicated and requires deeper contributions but the decision needs to be expedited

Consent: when it is important that people are actively part of the process and the focus is on action

Consensus: when unanimous support is necessary and the focus is on relationships

The first two methods are well known, but a brief overview of the last three methods follows.

"Advice process" is a term coined by the power company AES Corporation. It is a process where the decision maker is required to first seek advice from (1) people who will be affected by the decision and (2) people who can bring expertise to the decision. With this advice in hand, the decision maker decides and is accountable for the decision. The Canadian recruitment company Fitzii uses this method for all its decisions. The company has a system called "radical responsibility," whereby anyone who sees an issue can act upon it using the advice process.

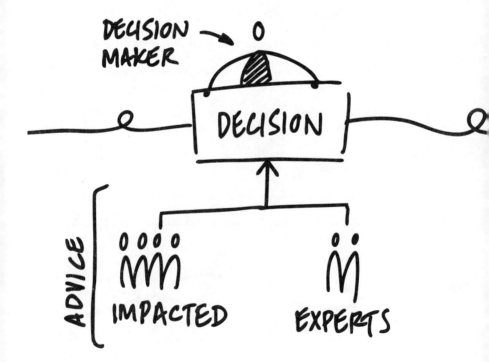

Consent-based decision making is a collective process that reveals whether there is a valid objection. It is about making decisions that are good enough for now and safe enough to try. There are different protocols for consent-based decision making, with variations based on the organization's needs, in how to develop a proposal and what constitutes a valid objection.

Consensus-based decision making is a collective process that requires everyone to say yes. Thus, everyone has veto power. There are protocols to help a group find full consensus, but reaching consensus can take time.

This is a practice of consciously seeking the appropriate method for the situation, opening up the question of what makes sense in a given situation. To answer that question, though, you need first to develop your skills in the full range of methods.

 Think of a decision to be made in your project, team, or division in the next week or two. Which of the five types of decision-making processes would you think is best matched for it? Why?

Clarifying When a Decision Needs to Be Participatory

Going horizontal does *not* mean that every decision needs to be participatory. Instead, it means that an organization is more deliberate and aware about what should be participatory and collective and what does not need to be. It is about being participatory and efficient.

To better gauge the nature of a decision, the following framework can be helpful:

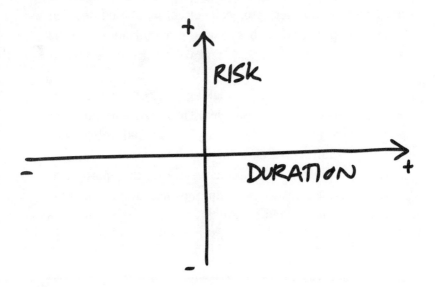

For example, say your organization is going to decide whether salaries should be transparent or not. Where would that go in the framework? The answer can be different for different organizations, and the framework can help in characterizing the decision.

The more a decision involves high risk and long duration, the more it should be collective (that is, made with collective input or taken collectively). The more a decision involves minimal risk and short duration, the more it is best left to a person or two. For example, two people should be enough to decide the venue for the next retreat. Even if the final decision is not the best, the impact on the organization is not huge.

> Identify four decisions that will be made in your team or organization in the upcoming weeks that fall in each quadrant of the framework. Then show the framework to a colleague and see if they agree with where you have put the decisions. The discussion can be revealing.

The other skill we can develop is learning to leave decisions to others and being able to live with the decisions that others make. Here are two questions you can practice asking yourself:

1. Is this a decision I really need to be part of?

2. If I don't participate, will I be able to live with the outcome?

Trusting one another for decision making is critical in horizontal culture, though it can be a challenge for those of us who like to have control. One thing you can do is to embed the two questions in your invitations. For example, you can explicitly invite those people who want to be actively involved to make the decision together, and those who can live with the result to leave the decision to the participants. By practicing in this way, you can start inviting a wider group, and people will come with more self-awareness.

In my organization I deliberately chose to not participate in making a decision after asking myself these two questions. Even though I was not personally in agreement with the outcome, the questions helped me accept the result. I then needed to make sure I did not override or undermine the decision that was made. I could make another proposal, but I could not undermine the decision. This part of the practice is important. You can always engage in a process to propose change.

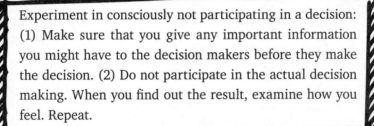

Experiment in consciously not participating in a decision: (1) Make sure that you give any important information you might have to the decision makers before they make the decision. (2) Do not participate in the actual decision making. When you find out the result, examine how you feel. Repeat.

Using Different Types of Agreement Systems

We can look at gradients of agreement in horizontal culture. Here are two ways of scrutinizing agreement, one from Sam Kaner in his book *Facilitator's Guide to Participatory Decision Making*,[29] and the other from the online tool for collaborative decision making called Loomio:[30]

Sam Kaner	Loomio
I really like it.	I **agree** with this and want to go ahead.
It's not perfect, but it's okay.	
I have agreement with reservations.	I **abstain** and am happy for the group to decide without me.
I have no opinion.	
I think more discussion is needed.	I **disagree** and think we can probably do better, but I will live with the decision.
I don't like it, but I don't want to hold up the group.	
I don't like it but will support it if I have to.	I **block** this decision because I have a strong objection and am not okay with it going ahead.
No way.	

Consent-based thinking shifts the standard question "Is everyone okay with this?" to "Is there anyone who can't live with this?" or "Is there anything here you can't live with?"

Instead of having to hear the details of why each person is in agreement, you focus the conversation around sound objections. Asking for objections invites everyone to get clearer on the distinction between their personal preference and the collective purpose. Some groups use the question "Is this good enough for now and safe enough to try?"

GOOD ENOUGH TO TRY...

WE HAVE NO VALID OBJECTIONS

I worked on a nine-month process with hundreds of participants who were co-creating a deliverable in an iterative way. We had regular co-design sessions with multiple stakeholders. Most participants were new to the project, so we began with a big visual display that showed the status of the work. Then we addressed (1) any clarifying questions, (2) what people liked about the work thus far, and (3) what they couldn't live with.

We weren't making a decision as such, but we were definitely ensuring that people coming into the process could truly connect with it.

The next time you (or someone else) asks "Are we all okay with this?" intervene to shift the question to "Let's ask ourselves: is there anything here that I cannot live with?" See how it goes. Understand that the first time you do this, people will still want to share their thoughts and ideas and why they agree, so you might need to be firm to ask to hear only sound objections.

Generative Decision Making

We now dive more deeply into a specific consent-based methodology.[31] I have chosen *generative decision making* because it blends both a strong protocol process with our human capacity to intuit a situation. Generative decision making requires someone to take the role of facilitator. When it is run well, the strongest voices are unable to dominate a situation, and forward movement is the focus. Here are the steps of generative decision making:

I. Readiness. Give time for open conversation for a proposal to take form.

 2. Proposal, version 1. Anyone can be the proposer, but the proposal belongs to everyone.

 3. Clarifying questions. The proposer provides direct, short answers or replies "not specified."

 4. Reactions. Everyone (except the proposer) shares their genuine reactions.

 5. Proposal, version 2. The proposer reformulates, completely changes, or drops the proposal.

 6. Objections. Objections are shared with the facilitator and discussed to see if they are valid. If an objection is deemed valid, it must be integrated into the proposal (new version).

 7. Visual confirmation. When there are no more objections, everyone signifies the same gesture to visually confirm that they can live with this decision.

The potential pitfall at every step of this process is that people talk too much. As social beings, we want to justify ourselves, explain everything, and provide context. Generative decision making is a protocol to save us from our usual habits and therefore needs to be facilitated tightly so people are kept on point and the process is not allowed to slip into the usual conversations. Carrying it out can take some practice. The full process is described in the appendix.

The first step, readiness, is important. A proposal can come from anyone and can begin by naming a concern. It doesn't really belong to anyone; it is simply a possibility that needs to be expressed out loud to help move the group forward. To get a proposal ready, you could offer a fixed amount of open discussion time in a meeting to allow the proposal to take form or have a small group spend some time exploring the options and formulating a proposal. The protocol can be used in official meetings and anywhere. You can be in a conversation or a work session, with no intention of decision making, and suddenly you sense a proposal taking form and recognize it as that, so you proceed with the protocol.[32]

I recently helped a group decide on a pricing policy in 90 minutes using generative decision making. We started with the first step, a quick check-in: "In the past few days what was a decision I took that was easy?" We shared and expressed why it was easy. That served as a reminder that we are all involved in easy, fluid decision making. Then I briefly introduced consent-based decision making. Then we had an open conversation on the question "What is the ideal pricing policy for a complementary activity offered at the annual conference?" I didn't intervene at all other than keeping track of the ripeness of a proposal.

Before the process began to feel tedious, I stepped in and invited someone to make a proposal. This is the second step. A proposer stepped forward, voiced her proposal, and began justifying it. I gave a gentle reminder that it was just about naming the proposal, no need to justify it. The situation was a complex one, as it needed to take into account conference-goers who had already paid, members and nonmembers, speakers, VIPs, and people who would want to attend the activity and not the conference.

The third step was a round of clarifying questions. I made sure that the questions related to the proposal itself and were not suggestions. The proposal had become a bit clearer by then.

In the fourth step, everyone voiced their reactions. This is when you find out how the proposal sits with others, whether they could they live with it.

In the fifth step, the proposer adjusted the proposal based on all they had heard.

Then came the juicy part, the sixth step, objections. These are objections that are not based on personal preferences. The goal is to move the proposal forward but to make sure you will not be causing harm to the organization. We dealt with a few easy objections. Two were integrated into the proposal, and one was retracted by the proposer herself after a bit of discussion. All discussion took place through the facilitator, which kept the group focused.

We thought we had made it through and had a home run until the infamous final seventh step, visual clarification. This round allows you to see if there is anyone who can't live with the decision. Sometimes a person might sense a problem but not yet have been able to put words to it. One person was unable to visually signify that she could live with the decision. We stopped, leaned in, and engaged in real inquiry about a difficult point that had not previously been raised. As facilitator I am learning how important it is that the person feels welcome to express themselves, not that they are a nuisance or holdup for the group but rather that they might hold some vital information that is key to this decision, and whose significance can be known only by exploring it together. With a bit of trepidation, the point was raised, welcomed, and discussed in every way possible. It took an extra 10 minutes, and in the end everyone could see that it was an important point to raise. The point showed that there would be impacts around the decision, and it had been a blind spot until then. The group gave their visual signification (raised thumbs) to express their joyful ability to live with the decision. The feeling was definitely that the decision was generative. We had just enough time for a quick checkout.

When people first discover consent-based decision-making, a question arises: What about the self-interested person? Would they not elbow into the proposer role, seeing that as the place of power? They could make a proposal that might even sound good for the organization but really be a cloaked proposal to benefit themselves. I reassure people that during the clarification round, this sham would be exposed. During

the reaction round, people are invited to truly speak their minds without anyone being allowed to comment. When a group of people sends a strong and clear message back to the proposer that the proposal is off track, the proposer is faced with two options: either disregard the reactions, or integrate the concerns and wisdom of their colleagues into the proposal. If the proposer disregards the reactions and pushes on with a self-interested proposal, in the objection step it will be objected to, because of concerns about the proposal within the group. All valid objections must be integrated into a new proposal. This decision-making methodology invites proposers to separate their self-interest from the organizational or group purpose. Those proposers who resist are exposed, and this can be challenging, even humiliating. These individuals will tend to either gain maturity or leave the group.

To build up to using this methodology, next time you are in a decision-making process, suggest to the group (even if it is just one other person) that you separate the discussion into *clarifying questions, reactions,* and *objections.* Make the suggestion as a way to have an experience of separating the process into the three things we do naturally that tend to flow into one another and therefore cause the meeting to drag on.

Making the Decision-Making System Explicit

At the workplace we need to know clearly where decision-making power lies, how you can get involved in decision making, and what decisions have been made. When this apparatus is not clear, it can cultivate frustration and victim culture (having to submit to decisions that you don't even understand the rationale for) versus cultivating a culture of agency, initiative taking, and shared accountability. Here are some basic elements of clarifying decision making:

1. **Types of decisions.** How would you classify the types of decisions at your organization? Decision types are dependent on the context in your organization. They might include, for example, project decisions, human resource decisions, organizational operations decisions, local governance decisions, and global governance decisions. Decision types are absolutely contextual.

2. **Accountability.** For each type of decision, who has the authority to make that decision, and who is responsible for it? The more horizontal a culture is, the more accountability needs to be explicit. Also, accountability for decisions tends to be associated with individuals, but it can be attached to roles that may then rotate within the organization (see chapter 3 for more on autonomy).

3. **Decision-making methods.** As your organization expands its decision-making methodologies to include advice process and consent-based decision making, it will need to map out the methods that are used in different situations. The organization will need to experiment before it becomes clear what methodology is best suited for a particular context.

4. **Where and when decisions are taken.** Which of your organization's decisions must be made in formal meetings? Which decisions can be made online?

5. **Documenting and communicating about decisions made.** Are the decisions that your organization has made tucked away in a PDF of the meeting's minutes, or is there a decision log that people can refer to? How are new decisions communicated to everyone?

What would change if a new hire in your organization were handed a map of the decision-making landscape at the get-go? What would that map look like?

> Take a few moments and try to map out the decision-making landscape of your team, division, or organization. Take your map to a colleague and see if they agree with the way you structured it.

Nourishing the Proposal Mind-Set

How comfortable are you at setting decision-making processes into motion? If you are a leader, you might be comfortable formulating proposals and making decisions. In fact, proficiency can be so strong that it might be difficult to see that others may struggle to do this. In a horizontal culture, everyone needs to feel the invitation, space, and capacity to sense a situation that could benefit from a proposal. For those who are not used to doing this, some stress or feelings of doubt can actually impede their capacity to bring situations or proposals to a group. Here are some ways you can intentionally grow a proposal mind-set:

- Offer trainings in sensing situations that might benefit from a proposal, formulating proposals, and asking for help to develop a proposal. You want to demystify the heaviness and bring making proposals back to creating something new.

- Track how many proposals people are making so those who are making them are conscious of that and perhaps begin to work with those who don't make them.

- Offer support and space to someone who would like to make a proposal.

- Remind everyone that when a situation is making them grumpy, that often means that they are sensing the grounds for a proposal.

- Invite someone to think through a proposal with you.

Vertical culture has accustomed us to a mind-set of needing permission, whereas horizontal culture invites us into a mind-set of making a proposal. This is a fundamental and comprehensive shift in attitude.

> If you are at ease making proposals, offer help to someone who is less at ease. If you are not used to making proposals, invite someone to help you make one.

Summary

Sharing decision making is about understanding your own fears and beliefs about trusting others and developing ease and skill with a wide range of decision-making methods. In this chapter we explored six decision-making practices that can be useful in your organization:

1. **Clarify when a decision should be participatory.** This is an art.

2. **Use the appropriate decision-making method for a given situation.** These include the lesser-known methods of advice process decision making, consent-based decision making, and consensus-based decision making.

3. **Use different types of agreement systems.** This can help you see a variety of methods that can make shared decision making efficient.

4. **Generative decision making.** This is a consent-based decision-making method that helps a group keep on track while separating personal preferences from the collective purpose.

5. **Make the decision-making landscape explicit.** By mapping the way decisions are made for all to see, you can foster a horizontal culture.

6. **Nourish the proposal mind-set.** Doing this as a conscious practice is key for a horizontal culture.

EIGHT

LEARNING AND DEVELOPMENT

Self-Directed and Collectively Held

*Learning organizations are possible because, deep down,
we are all learners. No one has to teach an infant to learn.*

Peter Senge

Going horizontal requires that people engage in learning and professional development to achieve this new mind-set, which involves shedding conventional vertical systems thinking and growing new habits and reflexes. However, the transition from vertical to horizontal mind-set aside, learning and development itself is a critical practice for individual and collective productivity and well-being. A non-hierarchical organization is by definition a learning organization that supports the personal growth and leadership of its entire community. It is based on the premise that organizations are as great as the people within them. Therefore, organizations themselves can and should serve as training grounds for us to become better humans. In other words, in addition to learning how to be part of a horizontal organization, you must also learn how to *learn* horizontally. Learning horizontally involves three critical principles:

1. **Self-directed.** Individuals are trusted and supported as adults to figure out learning that is good for them and for the organization.

2. **Egalitarian.** Everyone is invited. Personal development is not reserved for the organization's "high-potential talent," but for all.

3. **Collective.** Learning is held collectively. Colleagues support one another in their learning. The organization has processes in place to enable this.

Horizontal learning and development creates conditions that engender enthusiasm for learning and increased engagement with the organization. Challenging workers to grow helps retain talented workers and functions as a form of trust and recognition of their skill sets.[33]

In this chapter we look at ways to take ownership of your learning and development, collective practices to strengthen your organization's learning and development, and options to handle evaluation and performance, horizontal style.

How We Are Already Learning and Developing in Community

"Don't bend your knees. You need to keep your legs straight," says my stepdaughter as she oversees my swimming technique. "Move your arms like this," chimes in her brother as he demonstrates the way to do it.

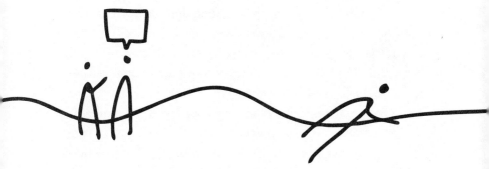

These children were offering me feedback that was timely, to the point, and clearly well intentioned—trying to make me a better swimmer. I decide if I want to take it in or not. I am free to offer feedback in return. Human beings naturally want to help one another grow and improve. We also naturally turn to our peers to help us learn. In fact, others can help us overcome learning barriers to access a personal breakthrough. Our peers help us with the juicy developmental stuff—self-reflection, awareness of our limiting beliefs, and evolution of our worldviews. Learning how to add content to a website, start a participatory meeting, introduce yourself properly—all these are easy enough. By contrast, the deep learning actually hurts, much as if we are injured or ill. That's why it helps to have support from our peers.

Take Charge of Your Own Learning and Development

You need to take charge of your own learning and development. No one will be able to nurture or champion it like you will. No matter how your organization approaches learning, nothing is stopping you from thinking and acting as the owner of your learning and development, here and now. After all, your skills will follow you wherever your professional journey takes you, and they will support you in other realms of your life. The way to start practicing learning and development in a horizontal way is to stop expecting others to organize your learning for you and take ownership yourself. Two practices to get you started are self-awareness of your learning needs and desires, and self-setting your learning intentions.

Create Your Own Learning Profile

In order to self-manage your learning and development, you need to be able to assess where you are and where you want to go. The best way to start is to identify your current competencies (knowledge and skills that enable you to act in certain situations), what you want to learn, and areas where you want to grow. This is called a learning profile.

Our needs and desires are forever evolving, so you will want to create your learning profile and update it every few months. Even if your work stays the same, your life skills are evolving. Since we grow from our life experiences, over seven years, your learning profile can completely transform. Competencies that you neither excelled in nor were interested in suddenly become interesting to you. Sometimes, you grow tired of a competency that you are strong in and no longer want to spend your days tapping into it. You evolve as part of your growth cycle. By letting go of a competency, you create space for new competencies to grow. Here is a tool to help you get a clearer grasp of your current learning profile and competency cycle:

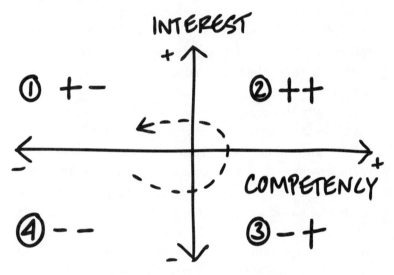

1. Competencies that I excel at but am losing interest in using

2. Competencies that I excel at and have interest and energy to make use of

3. Competencies I am not so good at now but I would like to develop further

4. Competencies I am not so good at and am not (currently) interested in developing

Most people will want support to identify different competencies that they can put on the matrix. There are so many types of competencies—relational, communication, collaboration, and technical proficiencies. There are also what we can call "horizontal competencies": productivity, initiative taking, conflict resolution, ability to live with ambiguity, ability to offer and receive feedback, ability to co-manage meetings, openness, ability to make decisions collectively, ability to treat challenges as learning opportunities. There are different frameworks, such as Future Work Skills, that can guide you.[34] To help you gauge whether a competency is a strength, think of an example when you used it in the past few weeks.

Normally, this competency profile will correlate with your work. An ideal work environment is one that allows you to focus mainly on the competencies that you are interested in using, are good at, or want to learn. Of course, at times you will need to tap in to some competencies where you excel but are no longer energized for, but you don't want them to represent more than about 25 percent of your work. If you are above 25 percent, you might want to think about whether the work that you are doing is right for you.

> Identify three competencies for each quadrant of the competency cycle matrix. Share the matrix with a friend or colleague and see if they can help you add a few more competencies. Outside perspective helps.
>
> What did you notice? Did anything surprise you?

Self-Setting Your Learning Intentions

When someone else is responsible for your learning and development, they usually determine what they want you to learn. When you self-manage your learning, you need to do this for yourself. Structuring your learning will help you capture learning more effectively. Bringing intention to your learning creates conditions for its development. The first and most important practice is to identify and name a learning intention, something that you would like to focus on learning.

Here are two examples of opportunities that lend themselves to setting learning intentions:

1. **A new project.** You are about to embark on a new project. What is making you nervous? What should you be paying attention to? What about the project is new for you? What are your limits you might reach with this project?

2. **A situation is grating on you.** This is usually an indicator of a growth opportunity for yourself. Examine the situation a little closer. What is it in you that is being challenged? How is this bumping up with a personal pattern?

Examining a context with questions such as the ones above should help you identify some learning intentions. For example, the questions might lead you to consider your own capability in facilitating meetings. Your learning intention might be to develop your capability to facilitate meetings. When you name a learning intention, it helps you tap into the opportunities to learn in your everyday work environment.

Learning isn't always about taking training; sometimes it is about sharpening your focus.

Document Your Current State

Another practice to help anchor your learning is to take a snapshot of how well you're doing on a competency. You tend to underestimate how much you have grown and learned, so a snapshot will help you gauge your forward movement. A snapshot is based on concrete experience. It involves documenting a recent moment involving a competency or learning intention you are focusing on that helps. What did you do well and not so well? If you have an opportunity to do it again, what do you want to be able to do?

When you do each of the exercises that we have covered in the chapter so far, you will create something called a "learning contract." A learning contract is an agreement that you can make with yourself to manage your own learning and development: (i) your learning profile, (ii) your self-generated learning intentions, and (iii) a snapshot of where you are now. This contract becomes a comprehensive snapshot of where you are, and it will help you take stock of your growth

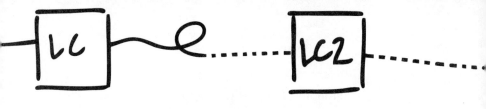

later on. It's a classic learning loop that you can create on your own. You can create a learning contract for yourself as frequently as you want. You might want to complete a learning contract at regular intervals and put that exercise on your calendar as a recurring event.

Identify a learning intention for the next month based on a new project or a situation that is grating on you. Take a snapshot of where you are now so that you can come back to that at the end of the month.

Removing Permissions

The practices we have been discussing are ones that you can develop on your own, or with a few colleagues, and propose for your team or organization when the time is right. But there are also ways in which an organization can support self-directed and self-managed learning.

Some organizations have completely released trying to control learners' training. For example, the director of a division at a European agency decided that managing people's learning and development was too time consuming and had a negative impact. His hunch was that people's learning and development would function better without management's intervention, so he replaced the old policy with a new one that required no permission for training activities. With this policy everyone had freedom and responsibility for their own training and could sign up for any kind of training, knowing that it would be automatically approved. Observers have questioned whether people would take unfair advantage of this level of autonomy. It is true that employees did take some unusual training that might not have been approved through the permissions process. Much of this training was employees exploring interests and future career paths. The policy was hugely appreciated by employees, however, and it significantly increased employee engagement with the agency. The freedom to choose their own training increased employees' energy for learning, so they took more time for learning.

Having to ask for permission to get training has a dampening effect on people's desire to learn. At Percolab every employee knows what their learning budget is and has full control of how it is spent. If employees want to design a learning expedition, attend an international retreat, or sign up for a writing workshop, it's all good. They are expected to share what they are doing with their colleagues and be completely transparent.

Having to ask permission to learn reinforces an adult-to-child culture. By contrast, choosing your own development path and explaining your reasons and rationale to your colleagues grows a culture of transparency and mutual respect. Shifting to a trust-based learning and development culture may not be easy, but organizations that are doing it are seeing a positive impact.

> In your organization what are the permissions required for people to be accorded time and budget to engage in learning? Identify a permission that might be unnecessary. Do you think your organization could experiment with letting this permission go? Identify training that would not be permitted where allowing it could be of value to your organization. Should this change the way the organization currently approaches learning and development? Do you think your organization is ripe to let it go?

Embed Learning Recognition and Rituals into Daily Work Life

Pressure in the work world can be intense. A project struggles because of your recurring blind spots. You find yourself engaging in tasks just beyond your comfort zone. A colleague gets offended and miscommunication spirals. You get inspired by a new discovery. Everyday learning opportunities abound, but we let them slip through our fingers.

Instead of focusing only on courses and trainings, we can embed rituals and practices that help us foster our learning and development from our daily work life. The value of learning in that way is twofold: (1) it's low cost, and (2) in the process the work climate benefits. Here we explore three practices that can help leverage that potential: sensemaking, feedback, and trigger logs.

Sensemaking

Sensemaking consists of practices that help people grasp all that is happening and extract meaning from the movement and chaos. It is a collective practice that helps turn the events of daily life into learning opportunities. Typically, the best way to engage in sensemaking is to home in on an event that has some type of intensity, emotional or other.

Here are three practices to enable sensemaking in a non-hierarchical culture:

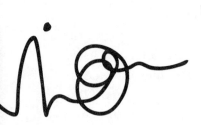

1. **Hunt for patterns together.** Forget blaming. Search for patterns you can uncover and name.

2. **Keep in mind that everyone has something to learn.** Engage as peers in co-exploration, even if someone wasn't involved in the event itself or has vertical power.

3. **Keep in mind that being uncomfortable is normal and healthy.** The priority can't be politeness. Learning requires hearing and exposing what's really happening. Insights come through discomfort.

Make sure that no individual has authority over anyone else in the process. To keep it a horizontal practice, speak of "we" rather than "you." Ask, "What are we seeing in what just happened?"

A slightly structured process can help with sensemaking. The questions below might seem obvious, but asking them can steer the conversation so that insights might arise. The structure avoids pitfalls of complaining or conversations that go in circles. Here are two examples of structures that could be useful:

Ask:

WHAT'S GOING ON HERE?

SIMILAR PATTERNS?

PERSONAL PATTERNS?

Ask:

WHAT WENT WELL?	WHAT DIDN'T GO SO WELL?
WHAT DID WE LEARN?	WHAT ARE WE TAKING WITH US FOR FUTURE ACTIONS?

Once you develop some horizontal practices, you will likely be more accountable to a colleague than a boss. Sensemaking will be important. Practicing with lower-stakes situations will help you prepare for the bigger ones where emotions might run high.

> Name something that has just taken place at your work—no matter what it is. Take a moment with one or two people to try out a sensemaking process with one of the two question structures.

Feedback

If you want to get better at something, anything at all, ask for feedback. If you want to be kind to your colleagues, offer feedback *without* the expectation they will act upon it. Feedback and learning and development go hand in hand, and fortunately you can practice it yourself intentionally whenever you want. Here are three principles to strengthen feedback in a non-hierarchical culture:

1. **Start with yourself.**
    Many people focus on how to get others engaged in a healthy feedback culture. However, the best way to bring about a feedback culture is to model it yourself. Modeling sounds so evident, yet it is a blind spot. You can craft your own personal question to invite feedback to get used to inviting

others to give feedback: for example, "Can you tell me two specific ways I can improve [name whatever it is]?"

2. **Frame feedback collectively.** Feedback can be experienced as something done to us, as a critique we receive. When we give feedback by framing it as a collective learning exploration, it is less intimidating and richer for everyone: for example, "What are we learning through these glitches in the onboarding process?"

3. **Find ways to deal with the discomfort.** Often, giving and receiving feedback can make us feel uncomfortable. Hence, we can find ways to avoid it or rely on others to take care of it for us. Rather, we should be finding ways to help us learn to give and receive feedback in kind and constructive ways. You could say, for example, "When you respond to my request like that, I feel shut down."

There are many methods of offering feedback, and each has value. Finding your ease at being candid, factual, and kind all at once when giving feedback can take years of practice. The situation–behavior–impact method described in chapter 9 is an excellent practice, as are others such as the radical candor method[35] and the four-step Rosenberg method.[36] Here is the basic format of the Rosenberg method:

Observations. State factual observations about the situation affecting you. You could say, for example, "Today is Thursday, and the work was due Wednesday."

Feelings. State the feelings that the observation has triggered in you. You could say, for example, "I feel angry."

Need. State the need that causes those feelings. You could say, for example, "Today is Thursday and the work was due Wednesday[observation]. I feel angry [feeling] because I trusted you to do it when you said you would [need].

Request. Make a concrete request. You could say, for example, "Can we take a moment to look for a solution?"

Another method is to use empathetic listening, the art of deep, silent, and open listening, for a fixed period. Person A gives feedback to person B for, say, 10 minutes. This feedback could be about a recent project or an ongoing responsibility. Person B listens silently for the whole time and at the end, no matter what was spoken, says "Thank you" to invite gratitude and learning. Then person A and person B switch roles.

You can integrate these practices into the workplace informally, or try embedding them more formally, for example by giving a standard amount of time for a feedback practice at the end of a team meeting.

Identify something you are doing that you would like to receive feedback on. Identify a person or a group of people you would like to get feedback experience from. Identify one of the methods above that intrigues you, and try out that method with the people you have chosen.

Trigger Logs

Keeping a trigger log is a practice that takes the feedback to a different space. With a trigger log, you record what happens when you have been triggered by an interaction with another person or a situation.[37] By *trigger* I mean a situation when something happens or is said that provokes a strong emotion in you, of any kind, that lasts more than seven seconds. If you can actually capture your triggers or reactions, you can enter a space of deep personal learning. The trigger log is a tool to support that.

The trigger log can help you uncover emotional self-protection actions that can be a barrier to personal growth. You can practice using a trigger log in an informal space where you feel colleagues are constructive and caring with one another. It can serve to move you through situations where you are stuck.

It might look like this: At a team meeting, take five minutes for everyone to identify three trigger moments from the past week. You write the context of the situation, a description of what was triggered, and an assessment of the intensity of the trigger. With a partner (preferably someone who was not identified as one of your triggers) share your triggers. Sup-

port each other's personal learning about the triggers with a question such as "What was it that triggered you? What are you learning about your triggers?" The question should be a supportive way of helping the person engage in self-reflection about the triggers.

This practice is self-directed, but that does not mean it's done alone. While many elements of a horizontal culture can be accomplished with just one person, feedback is something we cannot do alone. A structured process like this can support groups in thinking differently about an issue in a way that mitigates the natural feelings of fear and insecurity that come with the territory. It allows the collective intelligence of our peers to be channeled to deepen our learning. Holding your learning with others helps us go beyond our personal limitations.

> Try out the trigger log with someone you feel comfortable with. Invite the other person to identify three trigger moments from the past week. Share your triggers with each other, and ask each other the supportive learning question "What are you learning about your triggers?"

LEARNING

|

WORK

Intertwining Work and Learning

A team or organization can embed the practices we've been discussing directly within its learning and development approach. By embedding I mean an organization can formalize moments within a work rhythm, recognize them as important, and see them as having value for individuals and the organization. Work and learning are more interwoven than we acknowledge.

There are ways for an organization to formalize and recognize embedded learning moments. I was part of a series of workshops in Canada that invited professionals to contribute their expertise and ideas to a co-creation process. A participant noticed that she was learning a lot about co-creation methodology and asked if the time could be recognized as professional development. These workshops were not set up as a training per se; it was work. However, in the process of doing the work, learning took place, and we made sure it was acknowledged and honored.

This intertwining of work and learning holds much potential for the future. "Learning programs" can be distributed, and light learning practices can be embedded into work days. A "learning circle" is one structure to help do this. A learning circle is a democratic peer learning process for a group of people who commit to eight learning meetings over a period of three months. It is built on the theories of learning by doing and transformation learning.[38] The opportunities for learning in day-to-day work experiences are the curriculum. Individuals are supported with some structural tools such as personal learning contracts, theoretical models, and reflection practices to ground the process. The focus is to increase self-awareness of the assumptions and beliefs that an individual might be holding, and if appropriate to evolve them. The process invites experimentation to help people learn to navigate complexity.

> Think of your last week of work. Identify one area where learning and development was happening for you. Take a moment with a colleague to talk about and strengthen that learning. How would you want that learning to be supported by your organization?

Revisit Performance Reviews and Indicators

We like to perform well and excel at things we do. With non-hierarchical culture, performance reviews shift from a process done *to* employees to a process that all employees conduct together. Performance reviews become more about learning. In many companies performance reviews are no longer a costly annual event but are a regular integrated process. Netflix is an example of a company that has made this kind of shift.[39] Netflix changed from formal annual performance-based reviews to regular performance-based conversations among employees as an integral part of their work. The company began with anonymous software but moved into signed feedback and face-to-face discussions. Individuals can have their own performance practices. In non-hierarchical culture, performance reviews take on two additional characteristics: the metrics are determined collectively, and performance reviews become a horizontal process.

Metrics and Evaluation Are Determined Collectively

The choice and formulation of performance metrics are important; the values of an organization are revealed through its performance metrics. For example, a company that uses compliance-focused metrics is very different from one that uses aspirational metrics. Sometimes companies use metrics just to appear professional. For the metrics to be meaningful, the metrics must be upheld. If the organization has too many metrics or they are too abstract, people will disengage, so it needs to find the sweet spot for performance metrics that support its goals. What is essential is that the people who are held accountable to the metrics can take part in defining and improving them. This is a basic principle that needs to be explicit to all. If you are not in a position of authority in your organization, don't despair. In general, even if people are not explicitly invited, everyone welcomes ways to optimize the system. You can still find a way to bring your ideas and experience to bear on improving performance metrics.

Performance as a Horizontal Process

Once an organization has some performance measures that are clear and co-created, it needs to shift from using the indicators as a punitive threat to using them to support people's development and growth. Organizations have typically used a process of performance reviews that have been done vertically. The organization thus has no practices in place to support it becoming horizontal. One approach to horizontal performance metrics is to have an organizational competency framework that uses peer-attested mastery. Peer-attested mastery means that the validation of "mastery" of a skill or practice is no longer in the hands of someone who has rank over you but from your colleagues. For example, if an organization implements a set of standard competencies, colleagues can offer peer evaluation of those competencies. A spreadsheet with about 20 competencies that are considered core to your working culture and domain can be helpful to implement this. Employees self-evaluate their level of proficiency on each of these competencies, and they also evaluate their peers. For you to show mastery of a competency means that at least three of your peers have attested that they think you are at that level.

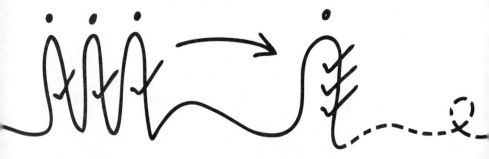

Another approach to horizontal performance reviews is to have participatory performance meetings. First each person should know which metrics are being used for the performance review. For example, at Percolab we had three performance indicators for the website: (1) employees feel the website represents the organization, (2) the website runs without technical problems, and (3) the website attracts more visitors each month. We invite each person to present the metrics they are accountable for and manage their evaluation process. For example, the web person would invite colleagues to rate their feelings as to how the website represents the company on a scale of 1 to 10. For the other two performance indicators, the web person would present the data to the group. In this way the accountability of the metrics is distributed among a team rather than held above the team.

As we discussed earlier, our three principles for non-hierarchical learning are self-directed, egalitarian, and collective. How do you do this with performance reviews? You begin by seeing performance reviews as a practice that can be integrated into people's day-to-day work lives. Next, you make sure that the same standards apply to everyone in the office equally. Finally, you make sure to include all the employees in policy and procedure decisions. All of this brings you into humility and self-acceptance as you start.

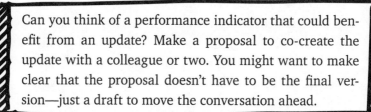

Can you think of a performance indicator that could benefit from an update? Make a proposal to co-create the update with a colleague or two. You might want to make clear that the proposal doesn't have to be the final version—just a draft to move the conversation ahead.

Summary

Learning and development in a horizontal culture is grounded on three principles: self-directed learning, egalitarian learning, and collective learning. Here are three key practices:

1. **Take charge of your own learning and development.** Invest in your own self-awareness of your learning needs and desires. Complete a learning profile and competency cycle matrix biannually. Self-set your learning intentions around a project or a situation. Look at how your learning and development program might be able to release a permission.

2. **Embed learning and development practices into daily work life.** Make your daily work life fodder for learning and development. Some ways to harness that potential are through sensemaking, feedback, trigger logs, and learning circles.

3. **Revisit performance reviews and indicators.** In a horizontal culture performance reviews are no longer a year-end activity that evaluates past performance but a co-created regular process that flows with the present and future of the organization. Performance metrics are co-created and used in a democratic way. The co-creation process can involve peer evaluation and collective evaluation practices.

In a horizontal workplace, the organization sees human development as an integral part of its success.

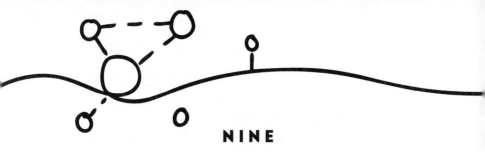

NINE

RELATIONSHIPS AND CONFLICTS

Tending to Them Together

The best weapon is to sit down and talk.
Nelson Mandela

Tending to Our Relationships
and Conflicts Is Important

Hierarchical culture is based on a parent-to-child mind-set. Managers are expected to handle disagreements and conflicts, play referee, and navigate interpersonal issues on behalf of their direct reports. This arrangement is convenient, in a way. It allows employees to take part as bystanders. It seemingly releases those involved from taking responsibility, and it allows for blaming others in situations of human complexity. By contrast, when you go horizontal, people are accountable to one another. If a person fails to uphold a commitment, that failure is dealt with among colleagues. No one is sitting back and waiting for a parental figure to solve all

the problems. In a non-hierarchical organization, each employee acts on behalf of everyone else.

What if our organizations helped us learn to tend to our
relationships better? What if work was where we honed skills
to be present, speak up, listen, and deal with conflict? These
skills are the cornerstone of life, and organizations need them
even more than individuals do. In order to distribute accountability and responsibility, it is absolutely critical to get good
at these skills, yourself, without relying on a manager.

In the hierarchical culture, conflict is treated as abnormal
or unhealthy. Workers find conflict exhausting and feel like
they are treading an obstacle course of human interactions.
But if we acknowledge that friction is part of life and work,
even embrace it as such, then we can begin to get better at
dealing with it, individually and collectively. This is when an
organization can really step up its capacity. The more people
attend to these interactions, the more chances are that fric-

tion won't hinder flow. This practice is one of the trickiest of all; after all, it is the life practice of getting along with others.

In this chapter we explore four key practices: (1) growing group relations, (2) being centered, (3) speaking up constructively, and (4) embracing our differences and conflict. A word of warning though: relationships and conflict are not easy. You will face challenges in this practice. We have been told that work is professional, not personal. Horizontal practices require you to walk a line that is both professional and relational. These practices can sometimes be confrontational and confusing. Adjustments in your practices will be required, depending on your position within the organization. These practices are hard in and of themselves. However, if you do them well at work, you will most likely also improve your personal life as well.

Growing Group Relations

We naturally value our social relations and make a priority of growing them. Our collective rituals such as graduations or engagements help to grow our relations. We know how to put a hold on our usual routines and acknowledge special moments with others. In a vertical work culture, a whole range of rituals such as happy hour and eating birthday cakes help us build our group relations. Team building, which has become a multibillion-dollar industry, directly contributes to strengthening relationships. Teams are given a specific challenge, like building a bridge across a river and crossing the river together once it is built. When relations among colleagues are strengthened, teams can weather storms and handle diverse challenges.

We first need to clarify what exactly we mean by *relationships*. A non-hierarchical work culture is all about seeing colleagues as fellow human beings who merit our respect and our support, but trying to be friends with all our colleagues is an unhealthy objective. Sure, some colleagues might actually be friends or grow to become friends beyond the work world. Making friends is lovely, but it is not an objective for organizations, and it is a trap that some people fall into. We must get beyond focusing on those people we have affinities with and open up to *all* our colleagues, in what William Issacs calls "impersonal fellowship."[40] The ideal is a place of mutual respect that does not always have to seek friendship.

We can now look at three ways of growing group relations at the workplace. Whatever your position in your organization, you can play a role in contributing to the development of the group relations. Some practices you will pick up quite naturally as personal practices, and others will be initiatives or proposals you will make for the group on a trial basis.

Little Rituals

If you decide that you will be growing the group relations around you, then there are all sorts of little initiatives you can embed in your daily work life. If you are going to sit down for a work session with a group, you can embed a rit-

ual check-in as a way for colleagues to see one another as humans. You might say, for example, "Before starting the meeting, how are you feeling about the project?" "How are you doing right

now?" "Is this project affecting your sleep?" "What do we need to know about one another right now?" These types of questions are not the focus of the meeting, just a premeeting moment to help everyone see one another as humans (see chapter 5 for more about meetings).

Onboarding Rituals

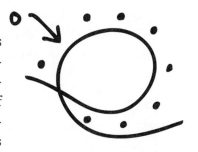

Onboarding a new employee is an ideal opportunity for building group relations. Most organizations make the error of doing it in a way that strengthens the notion of employees being friends at work, such as going for a team meal together. Having a meal together as a team is a great idea if a little process supports it being a moment that contributes to group relations. Here are some questions that everyone can answer: "How did you come to join the company?" "When is a moment you were proud to be part of this company?" "What is something about the company that others might not know?" "What is a project you worked on that you really enjoyed?" You get the idea. You keep the conversation connected to work, although not about productivity.

At Percolab we are process designers, so we developed an onboarding ritual we really enjoy. It can be played at the office or during a team lunch. It goes like this:

- The new recruit picks someone to ask a question on their behalf.

- The person who was picked thinks of a question to ask *on behalf of* the new person. They might ask, for example, "What is a tension you are living with?" or "What is your favorite kind of project?"

- Everyone takes a turn to answer the question as if they were the new person. The new recruit holds back from commenting!

- When everyone has had a turn to express themselves, the new person, who has been listening and keeping thoughts to themselves, announces which answer was the closest to what they would have answered.

In this way, everyone gets to know a little bit about the new person, and, at the same time, about the others in the team, how they think, how they are perceiving the new person.

Onboarding a new employee is an opportunity to propose some kind of sharing that contributes to the group relations for everyone.

Team Retreats

If you want your organization to foster better relationships, a retreat can help get you there. Organizations that are not building their group relations are paying the cost. This cost shows up

when people are distracted by relational tensions and un-spoken issues. Because of the stress, people may need time away from work or even leave the organization, leading to costly hiring processes and learning curves. Team retreats are a way to proactively keep group relations healthy, while allowing ideas and energies to come forward. By retreat I do not mean time spent together socially or time spent solely on organizational strategy. I mean a spacious period in which anyone can bring up latent issues, concerns, and ideas to be discussed and explored together in some kind of shared experience.

Here are some examples of activities that offer a light structure to keep the group focused on work, but with a retreat feeling:

- Everyone names something (workplace related) that they are grateful for (say in the past three months) and something that needs to be addressed.

- Everyone shares what they would like to accomplish by the end of the retreat.

- Everyone does structured writing or brainstorming to think about a concern or issue. Then they share their thoughts out loud with another person.

- Everyone identifies ideas they have or possibilities they see. Then people break up into small groups to explore the ideas. (No one needs to know about this activity in advance.)

- At the beginning of a hike, canoe voyage, bike ride, or other activity, everyone is invited to consider a strategic topic or issue, then sit with it informally. Upon arrival at the summit or destination, everyone discusses the topic. This activity brings fresh ideas and spaciousness to the topic.

- Everyone cooks together.

In retreat space everyone in the group has the opportunity to delve deeper into issues that are important to them. People get to deal with the things that daily operations don't allow time for. Being in nature can be helpful as a way to support the process because people tend to be more relaxed.

According time to the group relations is the groundwork that supports the three next practices, which are even more challenging in the work world—so you can think of it as a wise investment.

Name three things your organization does that contribute to building its group relations.

Identify a relationship-building opportunity in your workplace that you could try out personally or informally with others.

Being Centered and Helping One Another Be Centered

We can't talk about relationships and conflict without talking about our capacity to be centered. Everyone has individual triggers. And everyone has their own way of getting back to center. I walk in the park to get centered, while my daughter works out on a treadmill with blasting music. People also have ways of helping others come back to center, whether it is by acknowledging a situation or offering a cup of tea.

When I was 20 years old and attending university, the university pub had a wave of violence. Despite having many bouncers on staff to eject the rowdy customers, the problem was not going away. An idea emerged that was simple enough, but radical for a pub: why not hire female bouncers? I was hired as part of the experiment of employing female bouncers. I remember how nervous I felt my first evening, worried that I would be the target of verbal abuse or aggressive behavior from drunken guys. On my first night, I saw how easy it was to spot the agitation as it arose. A situation might arise from a jab poorly taken, a word misunderstood, a challenge. I didn't just wait at the door—I sidled up to the agitated table, beside the most agitated person, and ever so gently put my hand on his shoulder. "Hey, is everything okay here?" This gesture and question were powerful. The situation immediately de-escalated, the agitation dropped, and everyone came back to a calmer, more present place. I never had to actually eject anyone from the bar. This is what we can do for each other at work. Indeed, a calming influence can transform a workplace.

A full-on movement is underway to promote mindfulness in the workplace. When we are not present, we make mistakes, we say things we might regret, and we waste work time. Companies like Google have integrated mindfulness programs and spaces into their workplace. Mainstream media outlets write about how mindfulness contributes to work culture.[41] Basically, mindfulness is a practice to develop our capacity to be present and aware without judgment. Developing our skills to be more present or to center ourselves is about becoming more aware of our inner state and eventually being able to develop a calmer inner state. Leadership training integrates this skill today with the growing acknowledgment that the skill is not just trendy but actually can significantly contribute to the workplace culture. In a horizontal culture we strive to be more aware of our inner state and mutually supportive to help colleagues get back to center. Being present is a collective responsibility.

What can this practice look like?

1. If you recognize that you are in reaction mode, name it out loud. You can say, for example, "I notice that I am reacting right now, so I will wait a moment before I respond."

2. If you notice someone else getting agitated and losing their center, you can say to the group, "Why don't we take a break?" Or invite a minute of silence so everyone can get back to the task at hand.

3. When you are the target of agitated words, you can look at the person and let them know that you want to hear what they have to say, but not at this time.

4. You can embed collective rituals at the end of a meeting to allow time to review your reactions and how you dealt with them.

Taking on "being centered" as a shared responsibility is not easy, but it is essential to functioning in a horizontal culture.

> We all lose our center at different times. Identify two reflexes you manifest when you lose your center.
>
> Identify one strategy you have to come back to center. Identify a strategy you have to help a colleague come back to center.

Speaking Up Constructively

I love anchovies. At a restaurant when my Caesar salad is served without anchovies, which are pictured on the menu, I don't hesitate to speak up. If only it were so easy to speak up in the workplace. Developing a practice of speaking up is key for a horizontal culture to succeed. However, you might be doubtful of your own capacity to speak up clearly, or fearful about how your words might be received and how they could potentially escalate the situation. Practices can help you deal with these concerns. Here we look at three approaches to help you speak up: (1) a communication model, (2) the situation–behavior–impact method, and (3) a way of approaching speaking up as a practice.

A Communication Model

We are becoming more aware that communication in the workplace is more superficial than authentic. Theory U is an inspirational model to understand four levels of speaking together: [42]

1. **Polite communication.** You do not ruffle any feathers and do not say what really needs to be said, either.

2. **Speak your point of view.** You express different views, debate, and try to convince the other person of your view.

3. **Dialogue.** You engage in a genuine inquiry whereby you try to genuinely understand the point of view of the other person.

4. **Co-creation.** A group enters conversation that generates beyond what any individual was bringing to the table or thinking. It is a complete shift from a focus on getting others to think like you do.[43]

The Situation–Behavior–Impact Method

There are simple situations that can grow into tense situations if your voice is not heard. Here's a typical example: An employer agrees to accommodate an employee who lives far away from the office by agreeing that she can work at home when it is snowing. Soon after that, she informs her employer that she is working from home because traffic is bad—no snow, just bad traffic. The employer feels taken advantage of. If no one speaks up in a healthy, authentic way, tensions can grow. If the employer orders a realignment or reprimands the employee, a hierarchical culture is reinforced. What if the employer instead expresses their discomfort, names the consequences, and puts the question back to the individual?

A methodology called "situation–behavior–impact," developed by William Gentry, could be helpful:[44]

1. **Situation.** Describe the situation, being specific about when and where it occurred.

   You could say, for example, "Yesterday you didn't come in to the office."

SITUATION

2. **Behavior.** Describe the behavior that was observed. Do not assume that you know what the person was thinking.

BEHAVIOR

You could say, for example, "You informed me that you weren't coming in to the office because the traffic was bad. We did make an agreement that you don't need to come in when it is snowing. We did not have any agreement about traffic."

3. **Impact.** Describe what you thought or felt in relation to the behavior.

    You could say, for example, "When you extend the original agreement about snow days into a new area without discussion or agreement, it makes me feel taken advantage of. It puts me in a difficult situation with the other employees. It makes me want to cancel our original agreement."

Once all that is clear, you can ask your colleague what she thinks is a fair path forward. Every day around us at work, tiny incidents happen that have the potential to grow into difficult situations if they are not dealt with in a timely way. At Percolab one day, an employee inadvertently deleted content from our company's website. I simply said, "Yesterday when you updated the events on the website, you deleted all the content on the right side of the home page, which is now empty. If a visitor comes to the site, they might think it is under construction and they might think we are not involved in any events." The employee did not take offense, and the situation was corrected. However, it turned out the employee was setting up a brilliant new system around events. Instead of putting the person responsible on the defensive, this method allowed for a productive resolution.

The Practice

What holds people back from speaking up? Often, they are concerned that they might offend someone or they are unsure whether they will be able to communicate calmly. In a vertical organization, employees can leave it to managers to speak up. But in a horizontal organization, the team becomes accountable and has the responsibility to speak up. Speaking up can be uncomfortable for many people, so it can be helpful to formalize a practice of speaking up. You can start speaking up as a personal practice and each week make sure you are communicating to someone based on the situation–behavior–impact framework. You can also propose to do it with others in a small group. For example, you could have a feedback moment once a week. Remember, this is not wasted time by

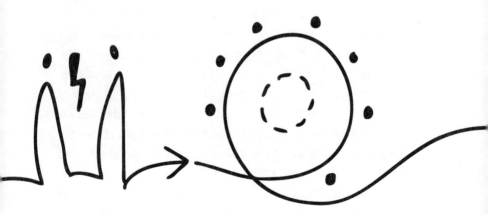

any stretch; it is time taken to proactively deal with small incidents before they blow up into more pervasive tensions.

Speaking up with your colleagues on issues of accountability is one of the absolute hardest non-hierarchical practices to develop. Looking a colleague in the eye and communicating in this way might not be easy at first, but it gets easier with practice. It is so much more constructive than vague statements about no one in particular that generate unease and misinformation. The table below shows the four types of communication: three traps that we all fall into, and the fourth type that is the constructive communication target we should be aiming for.

Human resources departments could be supporting the shift to non-hierarchical ways by helping people develop practices to speak up on issues of accountability. Developing this practice is critical for the well-being of organizations, and until that happens, the entire horizontal culture will struggle to grow.

> Think of a situation that is bothering you at your organization. Write down the basic facts about the situation and the consequences from the angle of the organizational purpose (not your personal preference). Now go to a colleague and speak up about this situation in a kind, clear, and constructive way that does not accuse or blame anyone. Then review the exchange: did it go better or worse than you thought it would?

Embracing Our Differences and Conflict

Despite what the media might have us think, we are by nature a peaceful species. We live with differences and disagreements all the time, more than we might realize. When we encounter conflict, we seek out the advice, wisdom, and support of others and figure out how to deal with it ourselves, without passing it on to others to deal with. I find it strange that at work we take our disagreements to our managers. Dealing with conflict is exhausting for them and not necessarily effective. We think that someone with authority over us is better suited to find the solution. By contrast, in a horizontal culture, employees deal with conflicts themselves.

Before we go further into the topic, I'd like to remind you that we should lower our expectations for constant harmony. Then we won't need to be disappointed, frustrated, and aghast when conflict occurs. Healthy disagreement needs to exist if multiple perspectives are to coexist. In his book *Collaborating with the Enemy*, Adam Kahane explains how the hierarchical way of dealing with conflict is all wrong.[45] We insist on clear agreements about the problem, the solution, and the plan. He says that instead we need to experiment with different perspectives and possibilities. We should let go of trying to change what other people are doing and be more willing to change ourselves. When we do that, we can get on with honing our skills at dealing with conflict. We discuss three practices that can help you develop your capacity to deal with conflicts in a non-hierarchical way. These practices allow us to share in the conflict management, rather than leaving it to our managers.

Acknowledge Your Tendencies around Conflict

A variety of frameworks and tools exist to support managers in their efforts to better understand and improve their approach to conflict. These frameworks are useful not only for managers but for everyone in an organization. One of these, the Thomas–Kilmann Conflict Mode Instrument, establishes five types of reactions to disagreements:

1. **Avoid.** You sidestep an issue or withdraw from a situation.

2. **Accommodate.** You neglect your own concerns and give in to someone else's point of view.

3. **Compromise.** You find a mutually acceptable solution that is not ideal for anyone.
   Compete. You pursue your own concerns at others' expense; you try to win.

4. **Compete.** You pursue your own concerns at others'expense; you try to win.

5. **Collaborate.** You work with others to find a creative solution that satisfies all concerned.[46]

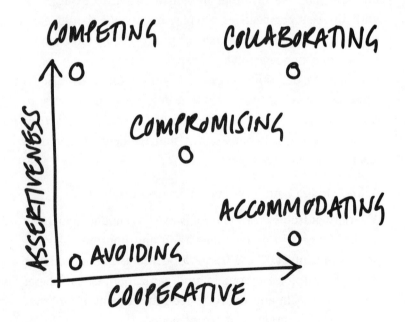

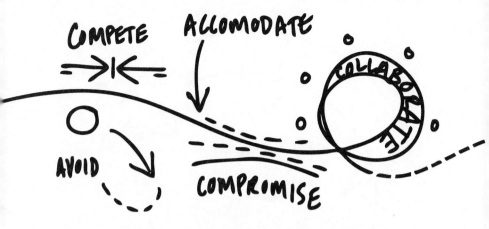

Your profile is based on how assertive or how cooperative you are. No type is better than the other because we need all types of reactions at one time or another. The importance of such a framework is that it helps us be more conscious of our habits around conflict.

What do you think is your natural tendency for dealing with conflict?

Identify a situation in which that approach has been helpful and another where it has not been.

Collective and Systemic Approach

In vertical culture, conflict is approached as a problem between two parties where other people avoid "getting involved." In horizontal culture the approach to conflict management is quite the opposite. Conflict is understood and dealt with as a systemic issue. A conflict "between two parties" is usually the expression of something wider that is going on. Naming it as a systemic problem shifts the focus away from the parties involved and looks at the underlying issues. It is a different way to approach what people call "interpersonal conflict."

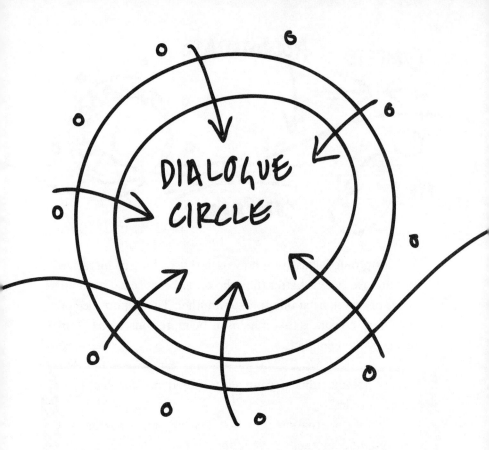

A dialogue circle is a simple and accessible technique to collectively address conflict.[47] Start by convening individuals who are connected to the system beset by conflict. If possible, organize the seating to form a circle because it avoids positioning the problem as a two-person opposition. Make sure you have on hand an object that can be used as a talking piece, some kind of object that will support conscious and respectful conversation: a pen, a rock, a ball; it doesn't really matter. This may sound a bit flaky within a work context, but I don't know of any other technique that is as effective for approaching a conflict systemically. Here are the steps to the dialogue circle:

1. **Welcome.** Explain why the conversation has been called and offer an overarching question or invitation that is inclusive to all and constructive as framing. You could say, for example, "How can we organize ourselves as we expand in a way that feels welcoming for new employees and caring for existing employees?" Also, get agreement on the duration of the discussion.

2. **Introduce the talking piece.** You might want to begin by acknowledging how odd a talking piece might seem, but then explain how truly effective it is to have respectful conversations that encourage good listening. When someone is holding the talking piece, everyone else listens with an open mind. When they have it, they speak from their own experience. They share their real thoughts and feelings. You can even offer a moment of silence if you wish. Everyone speaks to the center of the circle. No side conversations are allowed.

3. **Talking rounds.** The first person who wants to speak does so; the talking piece is then passed around the circle to allow everyone to give their perspective on the issue. People are able to hear others and be heard themselves, and to have their certainties questioned.

4. **Closing.** You finish with a last round in which people express appreciation or thoughts on forward movement.

Some people feel uncomfortable with the circle process, so you might need to just let them know that it is normal to feel that way and then continue.

Imagine a conflict around a project that goes over budget. If this situation is causing conflict, it is probably connected to a wider theme. Instead of meeting with just the people who are involved in the conflict, you can widen the discussion by asking, "What do we do when a project goes over budget?"

and invite everyone in the organization. By so doing, you make it not one side against the other but a place of collective inquiry. Sometimes this type of exploration can lead to a new proposal to update an organizational principle. By addressing conflicts in this way, you can optimize the organization's design and processes.

> Identify a situation that is current and not too high risk. Invite people to a conversation to unblock the situation, making sure that those people who are part of the situation are invited in a low-key way. Hold a collective circle based on the four principles above. You may find it a bit scary the first time, but you will survive.

Heal Emotional Wounds

When conflict occurs, you need to heal the emotional wounds. We do that well in our personal lives—by sharing food or gifts or a special moment after a conflict, as a way to restore the relationship. At work we don't need to reestablish friendships because we are colleagues, but we do need to heal the emotional wounds caused by conflict. If we don't make the restorative gesture, we can damage the organization's capacity to deal with difference and disagreement in the future. The healing process does not have to be extensive, but it should involve some kind of ritual to rebalance the heart, a gesture of kindness that restores, possibly by sharing food. These simple ways to reconnect cannot be neglected.

Summary

The skills of being present, speaking up, listening, and dealing with conflict are cornerstones to healthy organizational life. You must develop these skills for yourself, to release you from having to rely on a manager. Here are four practices you can do to develop them:

1. **Grow group relations.** Invest in activities and rituals, check-ins at meetings, onboarding rituals, retreats, that help people really see the other human beings we work with.

2. **Be present and help one another be present.** Staying centered is key to dealing with any difficult situation. It helps to have the support of others to do this.

3. **Speak up constructively.** When you notice something is amiss, you have the responsibility to speak up. Your focus is to serve the purpose of the organization, not to give in to your fears.

4. **Acknowledge your tendencies around conflict.** Do you tend to collaborate on creative solutions, or do you avoid, accommodate, compromise, or compete?

5. **Collective and systemic approach to conflict.** A circle dialogue is a safe environment in which to go beyond defending opposing positions and invite in deeper insights and thinking.

6. **Heal emotional wounds.** Rituals of healing can restore the group relations.

TEN

WHERE DO YOU GO FROM HERE?

Tapping In to the Opportunities That Surround You

A person who never made a mistake never tried anything new.
Albert Einstein

Developing Your Practice

The goal of this chapter is to help you get started growing your and your organization's non-hierarchical practices. Remember, the place to start is with yourself. Rather than worrying about what others should be doing, you can be more constructive by focusing on what you might be doing. You can follow this book in either a linear fashion or a more random fashion by trying techniques from any chapter. As you identify your own opportunities to transition to a more horizontal mind-set, you will want to look at each chapter.

Given that non-hierarchical culture is as much about the practices and the mind-set as it is about structural and policy changes, you can begin anytime, anywhere. This chapter presents a five-step process that you can use to identify and develop practices that will work within your specific work environment and context. All the practices interconnect, but deliberately focusing on one practice at a time is a way to support deeper learning and development. You will identify some collaborative, co-creative, participatory seeds you want to grow and then move into action, without overthinking it. Remember, practice, practice, practice is the key; by doing the practice you move forward.

Step 1: Identify a Practice to Focus On

Now that you are familiar with the seven practice domains in this book, you need to figure out where to focus your attention. Here is how you can get there: (a) a *self-assessment* to see where your needs are, (b) a *workplace scan* to see up-

coming opportunities for you to practice, and (c) *identify a practice* to focus on by mixing your self-assessment with your workplace scan.

The process will give you the clarity you need to decide which practice to focus on. If you already know, feel free to skip to the end of this step and record the practice there.

The self-assessment follows on the next page. I suggest you take 5 to 10 minutes to complete it. If you are reading this book with other people at work, you might want to all do it at the same time and compare your results afterward.

For each practice domain, rate your personal skill and ease and that of your team or organization. This assessment identifies the practice domains where you have ease and skill and where you do not.

Your focus on practice domains should be timely and useful for your workplace. Complete a workplace scan to identify naturally occurring situations and opportunities in your work where you could implement a horizontal practice.

Self-Assessment of Horizontal Domains of Practice

Non-hierarchical practice domains	Skill and ease 0 to 10 (10 is high)	
	personal	team/ org
Autonomy. Self-manage when, where, and how you work: focus on the organization, acknowledge challenging habits, and state your limits. Let others determine their own tasks. Help remove permissions. Take responsibility and action for what you notice. Adopt an attitude of stewardship. Hold yourself and others accountable.	_____	_____
Purpose. Make purpose clear in everything you are involved in: invite with clear purpose, take action to keep purpose on track, be self-aware of your alignment with purpose, and accept, intervene, or move on when you aren't.	_____	_____
Meetings. Take responsibility for collaborative and fair process and participation in meetings. Step up or down (as appropriate) to set agendas wisely, support self-determined attendance, and share the organization, documentation, and facilitation of meetings.	_____	_____
Transparency. Default to open with information, ideas, methods, and errors, and make access and use of documentation easy for others. Make your daily activities visible to others. Invite in the external world. Help to increase the transparency of budgets, bookkeeping, profits and pricing, and salaries.	_____	_____
Decision making. Match the situation to the decision-making method, clarify what needs to be participatory, use different agreements systems. Let others make decisions and honor the outcomes, make the decision-making landscape known to all, nourish a proposal mind-set for yourself and others.	_____	_____

(continued)

Learning and development. Own and know your own learning needs and desires. Help remove permissions required for learning. Engage in and initiate embedded learning rituals (sensemaking, feedback, trigger logs) and processes. Co-create, track, and use metrics.   _____ _____

Relationships and conflict. Grow the group relations, be centered and help others be centered, speak up constructively, be self-aware of your conflict tendencies, approach conflict systemically, and heal emotional wounds. You might notice that for some practices there is a gap between your capacity and ease and that of your team. This might be an interesting area to focus on.   _____ _____

A workplace scan helps to see what are the natural opportunities that you might want to tap into at your work.

Workplace Scan

Focus on the upcoming weeks

What project or event is starting or happening?

What project or event is ending or coming to a close?

Where and with whom do you feel trust and mutual support?

Where do you feel there is energy? Tension?

What policy needs attention?

What two opportunities in the workplace are catching your attention?

1.

2.

Now, let's put it all together. When you are able to see both your self-assessment needs and your workplace opportunities, you can choose the practice you want to focus on. For example, if a new project is starting up, it could be a good time to clarify its purpose. Or if a meeting is coming up where you will be among people with whom you have long-standing and trusting relationships, that could be a good place to practice starting a meeting with a check-in or bringing in feedback. If you are struggling to identify a specific practice within a practice domain, you might want to revisit the relevant chapter and see what inspires you.

Which practice will you focus on, and where will you do it?

Practice domain:

Practice:

Where and when in your workplace:

Step 2: Prepare Your Practice

Now that you know which practice and where and when, it is time to prepare the practice. To prepare it, you need to clarify (1) if it is a personal, informal, or trial practice, (2) how many times you will commit to do it, and (3) the current state of your practice.

You will want to perform the practice with others in an environment where you don't put yourself, your job, or your professional reputation at risk. Here are the three levels of practice:

1. **Personal practices.** Practices that you can perform without even naming them out loud to others

2. **Informal practices.** Practices that involve the participation of others whom you trust

3. **Trial practices.** More-formal practices that you perform as a trial with prior agreement with a group

I highly suggest that you begin in one of the first two practice spaces. Then when you're ready, you can perform the practice in the third space. Remember to practice non-hierarchical habits and reflexes to strengthen your ability to better bring them to others from a place of lived experience.

No matter the type of practice you do, you will need to perform it multiple times. Each attempt—whether it is a success or not—is an opportunity to learn and gain insight about what you might do better next time. After all, practice is about repeating the performance multiple times. By being clear and explicit with yourself about how many times you will commit to repeating your new practice, you will steer clear of doing something once or twice and then giving up.

Practice

What will be your practice space: personal practice, informal practice or trial practice?

How many times do you commit to performing it?

If you document your current level of ability on this practice, it can help anchor and strengthen your development. Each context is different, but some basic questions can guide you.

Examine your own behavior—not the behavior of others—regularly, for example, once a week. Think about specific moments and engage in self-reflection. On the following page is a tool to help you with it.

Current State of Your Practice

Over the past few weeks, how well have you been performing the practice you are focusing on? Put an **X** on each spectrum to indicate your answer.

1. What is your comfort level with sharing the current state of your practice?

   Keep
   private <————————————————————> Inform
   everyone

2. What is your emotional state? Where would you put it on the following spectrum?

   Charged <————————————————————> Calm

3. What is your focus? Where would you put it on the following spectrum? Consequences for:

   Self <————————————————————> All

4. How would you assess your accountability? Where would you put it on the following spectrum?

   Others <————————————————————> I am

5. Where is your attitude? Where would you put it on the following spectrum?

   Judgment <————————————————————> Inquiry

Step 3: Invite Others In

As you move into implementation, you will need to think through the involvement of others. Practicing in community is ideal, but the practice, the environment, and your level of ease and skill will influence how you will be inviting others in. In some cases you might simply announce that you are going to do something, while in others you would want to have a proper proposal and agreement with others. Here are five options for how you invite others in:

1. **Say nothing.** When the practice is more about something you will be changing in your behavior and you do not need permission, you do not need to say anything.

2. **Inform others.** When you do not need permission but you wish others to be aware of the practice, you can inform them.

3. **Informally invite.** When you want individuals to decide if they will take part or not, you can informally invite them.

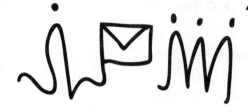

4. **Formally invite.** When you want the practice to be explicitly tracked by others so that it might eventually be adopted, it is imperative that individuals be able to decide if they will take part or not, so the activity will be scheduled, and you can formally invite them.

5. **Propose and decide together.** When you need a group to agree to try out something together, you propose a trial practice.

Invitation

Identify the type of invitation that you will use:

Draft the invitation here:

If you do require an invitation, remember that for the invitation to be genuine, you need to be ready for people to say no, and you need to let people know this. This is not a detail: The entire premise of non-hierarchical culture is to allow people their agency. Soft power is inherent in an invitation, even if the invitation lacks the hard power of coercion.[48] Once you have drafted your invitation, check it by asking these questions:

1. Is the invitation formulated in a way that the practice is portrayed in a positive light? Sometimes people defend a horizontal practice as though something is being lost with this new practice.

2. Is the invitation formulated in a way that it does not judge people or the current methodologies?

3. Is the invitation formulated in a way that makes the purpose of the practice clear?

If an invitation is required, find a time and place to deliver it. Once you are ready to go, you can step into the practice itself.

Step 4: Practice—Participate and Lead

If you are doing your trial practice where you need to invite others, no matter how informally, you will have a double role to play. You will need to participate yourself *and* engage others in the process. You will be participating, but at the same time you will need to keep an eye out for things you might need to do. This can be called "host leadership," whereby you are actively participating while at the same time exercising your leadership (which can come with a spotlight on you).

This dual role is in itself a non-hierarchical practice. You are on the front stage, back stage, and side stage all at once.

Practice Notes

If you are a manager, remember that your voice has more influence than you realize, so you might need to remind yourself to be silent at times. If you are not a manager, part of your practice might be to speak up or take accountability where you are not used to doing that. You know yourself and your habits and what you need to keep in check. You might want to write your thoughts down.

Remember, this is practice. You don't have to get it right on the first attempt. You will try, stumble, reassess, and try again. Despite your enthusiasm for going horizontal, you have non-hierarchical reflexes and habits that are still deeply ingrained in your mind-set, so you may experience tension, or even contradiction, between your ideals and your habits.

Step 5: Reflect and Learn

Reflection and iteration are absolutely critical to the process of transitioning to a horizontal culture. Practicing is about learning, and this is done much better with others than alone. Thinking together is what generates deep change. When you are meeting with others to reflect about a practice's effectiveness, everyone should prepare by looking back to the original goals and proposals, and the group should refer back to those proposals to support the reflection process. Referring back to all that you made explicit when you were preparing the practices will help anchor the reflections.

Interestingly, self-reflection can sometimes be even stronger with a collective debriefing, rather than an individual one. Providing an informal invitation to the debriefing session embodies many practices of non-hierarchy; it is open, and it helps people make sense of what happened. The debriefing should provide a genuine space for sensemaking and inquiry, not for pushing preconceived ideas.

Whichever method you wish to use for the debriefing, I suggest that you include some lines of inquiry that focus on strengthening horizontal ways of working: hierarchical bias, personal leadership, invitation, power, trust. Each of these ways of working can be explored in relation to your own inner journey, and in relation to the others around you, for the present and for the future. Here are five themes that can help work through deep-seated worldviews and habits that hierarchical culture has instilled in us:

1. **Hierarchical bias.**
   We are used to
   thinking that the
   hierarchical way of
   working is the only
   way, and we expect
   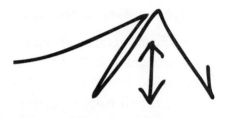
   an experiment with a horizontal practice to perform as
   well from the get-go as hierarchical practices that have
   been fine-tuned for decades. Did you notice your mind
   struggling with this concept? Can you name a specific
   situation where you noticed this happening?

2. **Personal leadership.**
   Where in the practice
   did you need to lean
   back and allow space
   for others? Where
   did you need to lean
   forward and take

   initiative and leadership? Where in the practice did you
   struggle? How well did everyone step into their personal
   leadership?

3. **Invitation.** It helps
   when non-hierarchical
   practices are brought
   in by invitation and
   proposal. How well
   was your invitation
   received? How could
   you improve the way
   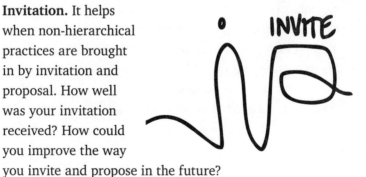
   you invite and propose in the future?

4. **Power.** Power flows
   vertically in most
   organizations and is
   attributed to people
   and roles. How did this
   experience affect the way
   power is distributed in
   your organization? Often,
   non-hierarchical practices coexist with hierarchical
   practices: how did both types of practices show up, and
   how were they navigated?

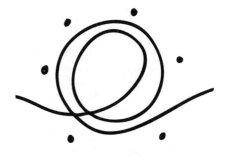

5. **Trust.** Hierarchical
   cultures are built around
   fear of human beings not
   behaving in service of the
   organization, whereas
   non-hierarchical practices
   provide light frameworks
   that help people trust one another more. How did your
   trust habits show up (be specific)? How were they
   challenged? Did you experience a shift around trust?

Insights

Identify two insights . . .

1.

2.

You can use these lines of inquiry in a sensemaking activity to identify learnings and opportunities for improvement. Clearly, not all of these questions need to be included in every debriefing. When you design the debriefing, consider your specific context: which of these questions will be most helpful for your situation? While people should have prepared before the session, starting with some silent journaling or reflection time to focus the attendees on the topic at hand can be a good idea. You might want to suggest freewriting or provide a prompt, but in any case the goal is to allow people the space to think about the conversation before they speak.

Practice, Practice, Practice

If there is one thing I want you to take away from this book, it is an understanding that going horizontal is about practice. Going horizontal won't be perfect or easy when you start— shifting your mind-set never is. It is messy and clunky, and it will require lots of checklists, trial and error, and pushing yourself. It is difficult not because it's unnatural for you—on the contrary you struggle because you are trying to understand and accept how you, yourself, have been upholding hierarchical ways for so long. It's like learning to drive a car: one day it seems almost impossible to remember to check in the rearview mirror every few seconds, and the next day you are doing it without thinking. This is what happens with practice. Something that feels so deliberate and takes such an effort with time becomes an automatic, effortless habit. This is the ultimate goal: to begin to sense your own role and agency, and to see the world of possibility. Go easy on yourself and others. The shift you're making in going horizontal is an inner one. When you think are you finished practicing, practice some more.

At the same time as you are strengthening your habits and reflexes and growing your horizontal mind-set, the world around you is continuing to change. The notion of co-creating more participatory organizations is slowly moving into the mainstream and gaining ground. The community of horizontal organizations is growing, the tools are expanding, the thinking is connecting, and the stories are making the rounds. Organizations can no longer envisage a future without greater autonomy and accountability for all, collective decision making, and co-managed relationships and conflicts. The future is human. The future is going horizontal.

APPENDIX
Percolab's Generative Decision-Making Process

Making decisions together does not have to be long and painful. The realm of consent-based decision making is not well known even though it can help organizations make decisions collectively, efficiently, and wisely. At Percolab, a consultancy company supporting social innovation and collaboration based in Canada and France, this is the process we use.

We developed the generative decision-making process, a consent-based decision-making process built on the integrated decision-making method of Holacracy with the culture and practice of the Art of Hosting.[49] We use it every week at Percolab. Our record is 19 strategic decisions in one hour!

The process requires a host; ideally, the host role rotates from person to person. At Percolab everyone can run this type of decision making, and we rotate by custom depending on the day.

When an organization first develops the practice, it can be helpful to invite an external host for an initiation or supportive coaching to develop the needed skills.

1. Ripeness

Is the time ripe for the decision? Is the context clear? Is there information or data that needs to be gathered? Could an open conversation help develop the ripeness?

> Hosting tips: You might need to offer the group one or two open-conversation time slots to get to this point (you could say, for example, "I am going to put the timer on for 10 minutes while you explore the topic in question"). Offer supplementary time slots as necessary. You might need to conclude that the time for the decision is not ripe, and that is okay. Listen in deeply, and when you sense that there is a possible proposal in the air, the time is ripe. Invite the group to head to the next step.

2. Proposal Version 1

Invite the group: "Would someone like to make an initial proposal?" The invitation will help the group move forward, and you will have lots of opportunities to fine-tune the proposal together.

> Hosting tips: Help the proposer name a proposal, ideally in one sentence. Avoid letting the proposal spread into multiple proposals. Ensure that the proposal is written for all to see (not just the proposer), and repeat it out loud.

3. Clarifications

Give the group the opportunity to ask the proposer questions. The proposer has two options to answer: (1) they provide the answer, or (2) they say "Not specified" if the answer is unknown.

Hosting tips: If someone is speaking without having a question (i.e., giving a reaction) remind them that it is a question period. Ensure that all questions are directed at the proposer and no one else intervenes. Avoid letting the proposer speak about anything other than giving a direct answer (keep it tight). Sense when the clarification period is about to end (i.e., when people are ready to react).

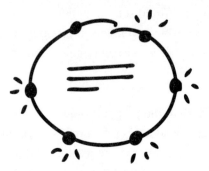

4. Reactions

Give each person (except the proposer) the opportunity to express to the group their reaction to the proposal; everyone's voice and perspective needs to be heard. The proposer listens deeply and takes notes. Afterward, the proposer will craft a new version of the proposal.

Hosting tips: Begin with the person who has the most emotional reaction, and then go around the room until everyone has shared their reaction. Make sure that the reaction is not about the proposer but about the proposal itself—step in if necessary.

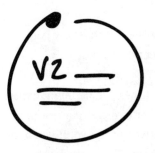

5. Proposal Version 2

The proposer formulates a new version of the proposal in light of all that has been said. Have the proposer write the new version, and make sure it is visible to all. Read it out loud.

> Hosting tips: If you feel that the proposer might want to stay with the original proposal, remind them that they can. If you sense that the proposer needs support in formulating the second version, remind them that they can ask for help—but do not rush into saying this.

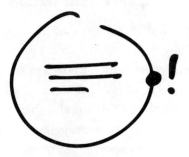

6. Objections

Ask for objections. An objection needs to express a risk or a backward movement for the organization or initiative. Listen to the objection and decide if it is valid or not. If it is valid, ask the proposer to integrate it into a new version of the proposal. Then repeat the objection round.

Hosting tips: Sometimes people might express personal concerns that are not in fact organizational risks. You need to differentiate between the two. If you're not sure, you may ask the group for help. This is the hardest part of the process for the host.

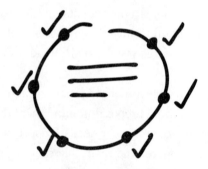

7. Visual Confirmation

Have everyone visually confirm that they can live with this decision by raising their thumbs. This is a way of allowing all to see that everyone is fully on board with this decision. If there is a concern that has not been raised, it will show up because a person will be unable to raise their thumb. This can happen when (1) the person is struggling to find the words to express an idea that is important to them, or (2) the person is disengaging from the process (i.e., holding on to the possibility of questioning the decision in the hallway afterward). Either way, the concern needs to be addressed, and the group needs to return to the part of the process that was not fully addressed.

Note: It is good to have a cultural cue as visual confirmation that a proposal may be fast-tracked. Someone makes a proposal, and you can just do a quick check-in right away to see if everyone can live with it.

Hosting tips: This visual confirmation is not a decision council, and it is not an opportunity to lower thumbs and restart a process. It is simply a visual confirmation. If the process has run smoothly, all thumbs should be raised. If someone is struggling to find their voice for an objection, support the person and let them know that all information is important.

A final word: just like when you're learning to play the piano, don't expect to get it perfect the first time. It does take some practice.

NOTES

Preface

1. Ulrike Hanemann, "Nicaragua's Literacy Campaign," Background paper (Hamburg, Germany: UNESCO Institute for Education, March, 2005).

Chapter 1. Why Go Horizontal?

2. Gary Hamel and Michele Zanini, "Excess Management Is Costing the U.S. $3 Trillion per Year," *Harvard Business Review*, September 5, 2016. In fact, the authors point out that there is one manager and administrator for every 4.7 employees in the United States.

3. Gallup, *State of the Global Workplace* (New York: Gallup Press, 2017), 22.

4. Jean-Pierre Brun, "Les Causes du problème. Les sources de stresse au travail," in *La santé psychologique au travail...*

de la définition du problème aux solutions" (Québec: Chaire en gestion de la santé et la sécurité du travail dans les organisations de l'Université Laval, 2003).

5. Ben Wigert, "Talent Walks: Why Your Best Employees Are Leaving," *Gallup Blog*, January 25, 2018.

6. Examples are Nation1099, a freelancer web publication, and SmartEU, a cooperative offering services to more than 85,000 freelancers.

7. Frederic Willequet, "Wirearchy: Sketches for the Future of Work," *Frederic Williquet Blog*, 2015.

8. Ana Manzanedo and Alicia Trepat, *Designing Positive Platforms: A Governance-Based Approach* (n.p.: Institute for the Future Research on Positive Platforms, May 2017).

9. Michael Chui et al., *Notes from the AI Frontier: Insights from Hundreds of Use Cases*, Discussion Paper (n.p.: McKinsey Global Institute, April 2018).

10. Buurtzorg was showcased in Frederic Laloux's seminal book, *Reinventing Organizations* (Brussels: Nelson Parker, 2014).

Chapter 2. Practicing Is the Path to Mastery

11. Benoit Sarrazin, Patrick Cohend, and Laurent Simon, *Les communautés d'innovation* (Caen, France: EMS Editions, 2017). People tend to stay in a community of practice when four conditions are present: (1) there is interest in the theme/purpose, (2) there is a place for sharing and growing, (3) there is trust with each other, and (4) there is no boss but self-organization.

Chapter 3. Autonomy

12. Sarah Brown et al., "Employee Trust and Workplace Performance," *Journal of Economic Behavior and Organization* 116 (2015): 361–378.

13. Elizabeth Hunt, "Pulling on the Self-Managing Thread: The Regitex Experience," *Percolab Droplets*, November 16,

2017, http://www.percolab.com/en/pulling-on-the-self
-managing-thread-the-regitex-experience/; "The Cookie
Factory: How a Burnout Led to Liberation," *Corporate
Rebels Blog*, April 3, 2016, https://corporate-rebels.com/
cookie-factory-rehab-turned-liberation/.

14. Based on a conversation with employees in Mondragon
in 2017.

15. Nicholas Bloom and John Roberts, "A Working from
Home Experiment Shows High Performers Like It Better,"
Harvard Business Review, January 23, 2015, https://hbr.org/
2015/01/a-working-from-home-experiment-shows-high-per
formers-like-it-better.

16. This is the European Agency for Small and Medium-
Sized Enterprises, https://ec.europa.eu/easme/en.

17. See Brian J. Robertson, *Holacracy: The New
Management System for a Rapidly Changing World* (New York:
Henry Holt, 2015).

Chapter 4. Purpose

18. Frederic Laloux, *Reinventing Organizations* (Brussels:
Nelson Parker, 2014).

19. Laloux, *Reinventing Organizations*, chapter on purpose.

Chapter 5. Meetings

20. Robert J. Stahl, "Using 'Think-Time' and 'Wait-Time'
Skillfully in the Classroom," ED370885 1994–05–00, ERIC
Digest, 1994.

21. Harrison Owen, *Open Space Technology: A User's Guide*
(Berrett-Koehler, 1997); and the Open Space Technology
website, http://openspaceworld.org/wp2/.

Chapter 6. Transparency

22. Wikipedia adds 20,000 new articles per month.
Wikipedia, s.v. "Wikipedia: Size of Wikipedia," https://

en.wikipedia.org/wiki/Wikipedia:Size_of_Wikipedia, last updated March 24, 2018.

23. The organization is European Commission, Directorate General Taxation and Customs Union, Programme Information and Collaboration Space (PICS), http://ec.europa.eu/dpo -register/details.htm?id=38627.

24. "Our Public Google Drive," August, accessed May 28, 2018, http://www.aug.co/steal-our-stuff.

25. "Steve Jobs Brainstorms with the NeXT Team," YouTube, 1985, https://www.youtube.com/watch?v=BNeXlJW70KQ.

26. Buffer transparent salary calculator: https://buffer .com/salary/senior-engineer-web/average/.

27. Some companies have been functioning with self-set salaries since the 1980s: Semco Partners in Brazil (with $250 million in revenue), FAVI in France (with 400 employees), Morning Star in the United States (the biggest tomato processor in the world).

Chapter 7. Decision Making

28. I developed this table for my trainings. Some participants felt that there could be an extra type of decision making added: status quo or nondecision.

29. Sam Kaner, *Facilitator's Guide to Participatory Decision Making* (San Francisco: Jossey-Bass, 2014).

30. Loomio is an online cooperative that helps groups make decisions together. See https://www.loomio.org.

31. There are many variations of this methodology: sociocracy, consent-based decision making, Holacracy, integrated decision making, P.A.R.S.E. (Present, Ask, React, Solve, Execute).

32. It is possible at this point to attempt to fast-track the proposal with a quick visual validation. If everyone shows agreement, then it is a decision. If there is even one dissent, the full protocol needs to be run.

Chapter 8. Learning and Development

33. Ben Wigert, "Talent Walks: Why Your Best Employees Are Leaving," *Gallup Blog*, January 25, 2018, http://www.gallup.com/workplace/231641/talent-walks-why-best-employees-leaving.aspx.

34. "Future Work Skills 2020," Institute for the Future, 2011, http://www.iftf.org/futureworkskills.

35. Kim Scott, *Radical Candor: Be a Kick-Ass Boss without Losing Your Humanity* (New York: St. Martin's Press, 2017).

36. Rosenberg, Marshall B. *Nonviolent Communication : A Language of Life* (Encinitas, CA : PuddleDancer Press, 2003)

37. Inspired by Robert Kegan et al., *An Everyone Culture: Becoming a Deliberately Developmental Organization* (Boston: Harvard Business Review Press, 2016).

38. Jason Seaman and Alison Rheingold, "Experiential Learning. Circle Talks as Situated Experiential Learning: Context, Identity, and Knowledgeability in 'Learning from Reflection,'" *Journal of Experiential Education* 36, no. 2: 155–174; Lena Whilhelmson et al., "Enabling Transformative Learning in the Workplace: An Educative Research Intervention," *Journal of Transformative Education* 13, no. 3: 219–238.

39. Patty McCord, "How Netflix Reinvented HR," *Harvard Business Review*, January–February 2014.

Chapter 9. Relationships and Conflicts

40. William Isaacs, *Dialogue: The Art of Thinking Together* (New York: Doubleday, 1999).

41. See, for example, Gill Crossland-Thackray, "Mindfulness at Work: What Are the Benefits?" *Guardian* December 21, 2012; and Ashley Stahl, "How to Practice Mindfulness at Work," *Forbes*, September 14, 2017.

42. Scharmer, C. Otto, *Theory U: Leading from the Future as It Emerges* (San Franciso: Berrett-Koehler Publishers, 2009)

43.   Otto Scharmer, *The Essentials of Theory U: Core Principles and Applications* (Oakland: Berrett-Koehler, 2018), 42–46.

44.   William Gentry, *Be the Boss Everyone Wants to Work For: A Guide for New Leaders* (Oakland: Berrett-Koehler, 2016).

45.   Adam Kahane, *Collaborating with the Enemy: How to Work with People You Don't Agree With or Like or Trust* (Oakland: Berrett-Koehler, 2017).

46.   Kenneth W. Thomas, and Ralph H. Kilmann, *Thomas–Kilmann Conflict Mode Instrument: Profile and Interpretive Report* (n.p.: CPP, 2008), http://www.kilmanndiagnostics.com/sites/default/files/TKI_Sample_Report.pdf.

47.   William Isaacs, *Dialogue: The Art of Thinking Together* (New York: Doubleday, 1999).

Chapter 10. Where Do You Go from Here?

48.   M. W. McKergow, "Leader as Host, Host as Leader: Towards a New Yet Ancient Metaphor," *International Journal for Leadership in Public Services* 5, no. 1: 19–24.

Appendix

49.   Art of Hosting (website), accessed July 3, 2018, http://www.artofhosting.org/.

BIBLIOGRAPHY

Bloom, Nicholas, and John Roberts. "A Working from Home
Experiment Shows High Performers Like It Better." *Harvard
Business Review*, January 23, 2015, https://hbr.org/2015/01/
a-working-from-home-experiment-shows-high-performers-like-it
-better.

Brown, Sarah, Daniel Gray, Jolien McHardy, and Karl Taylor.
"Employee Trust and Workplace Performance." *Journal of Economic
Behavior and Organization* 116 (2015): 361–378.

Hanemann, Ulrike. "Nicaragua's Literacy Campaign." Background
paper. Hamburg, Germany: UNESCO Institute for Education,
March 2005.

Kaner, Sam. *Facilitator's Guide to Participatory Decision Making*.
Community at Work, 2014.

Kegan, Robert, Lisa Laskow Lahey, Matthew L. Miller, and
Andy Fleming. *An Everyone Culture: Becoming a Deliberately*

Developmental Organization. Boston: Harvard Business Review Press, 2016.

Laloux, Frederic. *Reinventing Organizations.* Brussels: Nelson Parker, 2014.

Owen, Harrison. *Open Space Technology: A User's Guide.* Oakland: Berrett-Koehler, 1997.

Robertson, Brian J. *Holacracy: The New Management System for a Rapidly Changing World.* New York: Henry Holt, 2015.

Stahl, Robert J. "Using 'Think-Time' and 'Wait-Time' Skillfully in the Classroom." ERIC Digest, ED370885 1994–05–00, 1994.

ACKNOWLEDGMENTS

Thank you to the many people who have helped make this book possible.

To my amazing publisher, which is on its own journey as a horizontal organization. To my editor, Anna Leinberger, for her participatory ways and so much patience.

To the Percolab crew for all the co-learning in our horizontal practice field, especially Nadine, Paul, Ria, Karine, Fanny, Ivo, Ann, Ilona, Nil, Hélène, Denis, Meghan, Chloe, Solène, Laurence, Ezra, Elizabeth, Cédric, Stéphane, Stéphanie, Lydia, Lucas, Dominique, Roch, Yves. To Percolab partners and collaborators with whom we grow, Hafid, Clémence, Monique, Raquel, and others.

To my family for allowing my work and personal life to ebb and flow, especially Yoann, Zoé, Reuben, Ava, Kim, Paul,

Adam, Jenny, Colin, Helen, and my parents. With a shout-out to my mother and her friend Denise for their curiosity and commitment to going horizontal.

To the international Art of Hosting and Flow Game communities for anchoring me, especially Toke, Monica, Ria, Nadine, Chris, Tuesday, Amanda, Sophia, Tracy, Melinda, Caroline, and Helen.

To Teal for Startups community, especially Susan, Brent, and Travis, for unknowingly provoking the connection with Berrett-Koehler.

To the growing self-managing organizations community, especially, Frederic, George, Susan, and Ria. To the Unleash community for the deep learnings, especially Dirk and Connor. To all the wild ones out there in New Zealand and a summer house in Hungary. To the Tiimiakatemia community for lighting a spark years ago, Étienne and Ville. To the McConnell Foundation.

To my friends for giving me space, especially Colleen, Bruce, Cathie, Cécile, Lynn, Pete, Melissa, Jean-François, and Patricia.

To Mark, our coach with a magic touch.

To Percolab past, present, and future.

To my colleague Paul for the visual whimsy and wisdom you bring to my work.

To my husband, Paul, for being by my side and playing in the water.

INDEX

Page numbers followed by a *t* indicate a table, and those followed by an *f* indicate a figure.

ABOUT THE AUTHOR

SAMANTHA SLADE is a social designer who supports teams, organizations, and ecosystems to grow their horizontal ways. She is the co-founder of Percolab, an international network of co-creation and co-design firms. With her colleagues and collaborators, she pioneers culture-driven practices and operational tools for the future of work. She has supported organizations in a dozen countries, including innovative start-ups and the European Commission. She also founded the co-working space Ecto. Samantha has piloted new business training formats and dreams of the next generation of business and management education.

For more than 20 years, Samantha Slade has been putting her background in anthropology and learning design to use in the service of innovation work with organizations. She holds a a graduate degree in learning design, a graduate diploma in teaching and a bachelor's degree in cultural anthropology.

Samantha lives in Montreal, Canada, where she loves to bike to her meetings and recharge by canoe camping. Samantha believes that organizations can and should be a microcosm of the world we want to live in.

Berrett–Koehler
Publishers

Connecting people and ideas
to create a world that works for all

Dear Reader,

Thank you for picking up this book and joining our worldwide community of Berrett-Koehler readers. We share ideas that bring positive change into people's lives, organizations, and society.

To welcome you, we'd like to offer you a free e-book. You can pick from among twelve of our bestselling books by entering the promotional code **BKP92E** here: http://www.bkconnection.com/welcome.

When you claim your free e-book, we'll also send you a copy of our e-newsletter, the *BK Communiqué*. Although you're free to unsubscribe, there are many benefits to sticking around. In every issue of our newsletter you'll find

- A free e-book
- Tips from famous authors
- Discounts on spotlight titles
- Hilarious insider publishing news
- A chance to win a prize for answering a riddle

Best of all, our readers tell us, "Your newsletter is the only one I actually read." So claim your gift today, and please stay in touch!

Sincerely,

Charlotte Ashlock
Steward of the BK Website

Questions? Comments? Contact me at bkcommunity@bkpub.com.